THE BASICS OF
HEAT

CORE CONCEPTS

THE BASICS OF HEAT

JOHN O. E. CLARK

ROSEN
PUBLISHING®

New York

This edition published in 2015 by:

The Rosen Publishing Group, Inc.
29 East 21st Street
New York, NY 10010

Additional end matter copyright © 2015 by The Rosen Publishing Group, Inc.

Library of Congress Cataloging-in-Publication Data

Clark, John O. E.
The basics of heat/by John O. E. Clark.
    p. cm.—(Core concepts)
Includes bibliographic references and index.
ISBN 978-1-4777-7764-0 (library binding)
1. Heat—Juvenile literature. 2. Heat—Transmission—Juvenile literature. I. Clark, John Owen Edward. II. Title.
QC320.14 C54 2015
536—d23

Manufactured in the United States of America

© 2004 Brown Bear Books Ltd.

CONTENTS

CHAPTER ONE

THE POWER OF HEAT

Heat is clearly a form of energy because it can be made to do work, as it does in steam engines and gasoline engines. Hot things possess heat energy, which they "store" in their vibrating atoms or molecules. The more these particles vibrate, the hotter the material gets. Particles in cold materials do not vibrate as much.

Energy comes in many different forms. For example, light and electricity are both forms of energy. Objects in motion possess kinetic energy, and even stationary objects have potential energy. In

addition every object contains some internal energy that lies in the small vibrations of the atoms or molecules it is made of. It is this energy that we call heat. More technically, heat represents the transfer of energy from a hot object to a cooler one because of their difference in temperature.

A red-hot nail is much hotter than a bucket of warm water. Yet the water contains more heat energy than the nail. The level of "hotness" is an object's temperature, and it depends on how vigorously the object's component particles—its atoms or molecules—are vibrating. The bucket of warm water contains many more particles than the nail does, and therefore it "stores" more heat, even though its temperature is much lower. Adding heat to an object will increase its temperature, while removing heat from it will lower its temperature.

JOULES AND CALORIES

Because heat is a form of energy, its correct scientific unit is the joule. Technically, 1 joule is the amount of work done when a force of 1 newton acts through a distance of 1 meter. All forms of energy—and work—can be measured in joules.

A grass fire quickly gets out of control as it is spread by the wind. It is an example of the potential destructive power of flames.

An older unit called the calorie (abbreviation cal) is still sometimes used to measure heat. One calorie is the heat needed to raise the temperature of 1 gram of water through 1°C. The calorie is a small unit, and often the kilocalorie is used in practice. One kilocalorie (kcal) equals 1,000 calories. To add to the confusion, dieticians who deal with the energy values of foods call this unit the Calorie (with a capital C); 1 Calorie equals 1,000 calories. Often the capital C is omitted on food labels. So a 200-calorie piece of candy actually has an energy content of 200 kcal—more than enough to boil 2 kg (just over 2 quarts) of water.

Sometimes it is necessary to convert calories into joules (or vice versa). You need to know that 1 calorie equals approximately 4.2 joules (4.1868 joules, to be precise).

Food labels typically give the amount of Calories in one serving of the food.

Nutrition Facts

Serving Size	1 Cup (53g/1.9 oz.)
Servings Per Container	About 9

Amount Per Serving

Calories 188	Calories from Fat 25

	% Daily Value*
Total Fat 3g	5%
Saturated Fat 0g	0%
Trans Fat 0g	
Cholesterol 0mg	0%
Sodium 80mg	3%
Potassium 300mg	9%
Total Carbohydrate 37g	12%
Dietary Fiber 8g	32%
Soluble Fiber	
Insoluble Fibe	4%
Sugars 13g	
Protein 9g	14%

Vitamin A 0%	C 0%
Calcium 4%	10%
Phosphorus 10%	0%

* Percent Daily Values are based o
Your daily values may be higher o

Blacksmiths use heat to shape metals. You can see the hottest part of this piece of metal glowing orange.

CHAPTER TWO

HOW IS HEAT PRODUCED?

Heat can be produced in many ways—by burning things, by using electricity, even by rubbing your hands together. You can also feel heat in the rays of the Sun, and deep underground is a source of heat from the very center of the Earth itself, which can be tapped to generate *geothermal power. Nuclear reactors also produce heat.*

Because heat is a type of energy, it is generally produced by converting other forms of energy. For example, when a piece of coal burns, the chemical energy in it is released as heat in the chemical reaction called combustion (burning). Chemical energy is converted to heat when any fuel burns and is often put to use in heat engines such as the diesel engine in a truck.

Another common way of producing heat in homes and industry is to use electricity. Electric heaters rely on the fact that when an electric current flows

The back tires of a drag racer spin at the beginning of a run. Friction makes the surface of the tires so hot that they burn as the car streaks away.

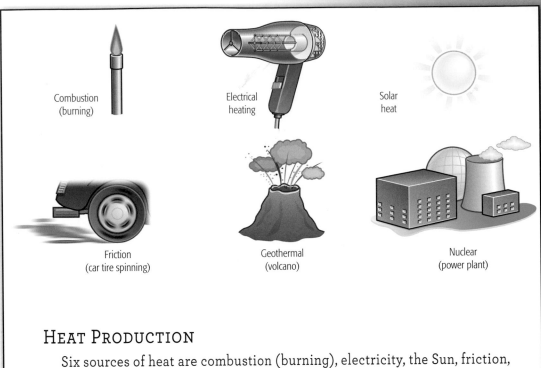

HEAT PRODUCTION

Six sources of heat are combustion (burning), electricity, the Sun, friction, geothermal (from the center of the Earth), and a nuclear reactor.

through a piece of wire, the wire gets hot. Special high-resistance wire is used, so that it does not burn away or get too hot and melt.

HEAT CAUSED BY FRICTION

The conversion of mechanical energy into heat was observed in the 1790s by the American-born British scientist Count Rumford. He correctly assumed that the mechanical energy of a machine boring a cannon barrel was converted to heat because of friction between the drill and the metal of the barrel. He even submerged the barrel and the drill in a tank of water, and after a while the water in the tank boiled because of the heat produced.

Heat caused by friction is a nuisance in any kind of machinery that has moving parts. Engineers design special bearings for rotating shafts to minimize friction, which can also be reduced by using a lubricant such as oil. Also, many drilling and milling machines employ a watery lubricating liquid that flows over the work-piece and carries away the heat produced.

COUNT RUMFORD

Count Rumford was born Benjamin Thompson in 1753 in Woburn, Massachusetts. The son of a farmer, he became an international politician and physicist. He spied for the British during the American Revolution and in 1775 went to England before moving on to Germany, where he became a count. Watching machines boring cannon barrels at the Munich arsenal, Rumford noticed how hot they got. He realized that heat is a form of energy produced by friction. After his return to England in 1798 he invented several devices, including a kitchen stove, an oil lamp, and a photometer (for measuring the brightness of light).

HEAT FROM NATURE

Various natural objects are hot and can give up some of their heat. Such objects include the Sun, whose heat you can feel with your skin, and the Earth itself. The Earth's core, at a temperature of about 4,000°C (about 7,200°F), is surrounded by a 3,000-km (1,850-mile) thick mantle of molten rock, topped by a rocky crust. By drilling down into the crust (which is up to 40 km/25 miles thick), engineers can tap the Earth's internal heat. Hot springs also bring this geothermal energy to the surface.

Blue Lagoon Geothermal Spa, in Iceland, is an example of geothermal energy.

CHAPTER THREE

MEASURING HEAT

We all know that something with a high temperature is hot. So temperature is the degree of hotness of something, which is a measure of how vigorously its atoms or molecules are vibrating. Scientists express temperatures on a temperature scale.

We know that if we want to make something hotter, we have to supply it with heat. It would be very useful if we could take a hot object, put it in contact with a warm one, and have heat travel from the warm object to the hot one—making it even hotter. But this goes against the laws of physics. One of these laws states that heat will not flow of its own accord from a cool object to a warmer one, only from warm to cooler. If we get too hot in the summer, we cool down by moving to somewhere that is colder—such as a swimming pool.

DIFFERENT SCALES

To measure an object's temperature we use some form of thermometer (see page 18). The thermometer has to be graduated in degrees of hotness. These graduations together form a temperature scale, and over the years various scales have been devised.

Even rocks and concrete melt if they are made hot enough.

Most have to have at least two fixed points, such as the temperatures at which water freezes or boils.

Two common temperature scales are named after their inventors. The German physicist Gabriel Fahrenheit, who made the first alcohol-containing thermometer in 1709, invented the Fahrenheit scale. On this scale the freezing point of water is 32°F, and the boiling point is 212°F. The Celsius scale was devised by the Swedish astronomer Anders Celsius in 1742. It has the freezing point of water as 0°C and the boiling point as 100°C. Since there are 100 degrees in this range, it was originally called the centigrade scale ("centi-" meaning a hundred).

Another way to consider temperature is as thermodynamic temperature, based on the motion of atoms and molecules.

TEMPERATURE SCALES

The chief temperature scales are the Fahrenheit scale, used for weather forecasts and everyday purposes; the Celsius scale (formerly called centigrade), used in science and for everyday measurements in most European countries; and the Kelvin scale, which is based on absolute zero. A Kelvin degree is the same size as a Celsius degree.

Fahrenheit °F	Celsius °C	Kelvin K	
212°F	100°C	373 K	Water boils — (100°C)
176°F	80°C	353 K	
140°F	60°C	333 K	
104°F	40°C	313 K	
68°F	20°C	293 K	Average room temperature — (21°C)
32°F	0°C	273 K	Water freezes — (0°C)
4°F	–20°C	253 K	
–40°F	–40°C	233 K	Mercury — (–38.9°C) freezes
–76°F	–60°C	213 K	
–112°F	–80°C	193 K	
–148°F	–100°C	173 K	
–184°F	–120°C	153 K	Alcohol — (–117.3°C) freezes
–220°F	–140°C	133 K	
–256°F	–160°C	113 K	
–292°F	–180°C	93 K	Oxygen — (–183°C) boils
–328°F	–200°C	73 K	
–364°F	–220°C	53 K	Oxygen — (–218.4°C) freezes
–400°F	–240°C	33 K	
–436°F	–260°C	13 K	
–459.4°F	–273°C	0 K	Absolute zero — (–273°C)

The lowest temperature possible is called absolute zero, which equals –273°C (–459.4°F). At this temperature atoms and molecules stop moving altogether, so nothing can be made any colder. Scientists measure thermodynamic temperature on the Kelvin scale, on which absolute zero is 0 K (notice there is no degree sign). On this scale the freezing point of water (0°C) is 273 K. A Kelvin degree is the same size as a Celsius degree. Temperature differences—as opposed to fixed temperatures—are often expressed in Kelvin rather than Celsius. The scale is named after the Scottish physicist William Thomson, who became Lord Kelvin in 1892 when he was knighted for his services to science.

Here a computer's CPU is cooled with liquid nitrogen. This liquid boils at –195.8°C (–352.4°F) and is used in engineering and scientific research.

Most common thermometers give measurements in both the Fahrenheit and Celsius scales.

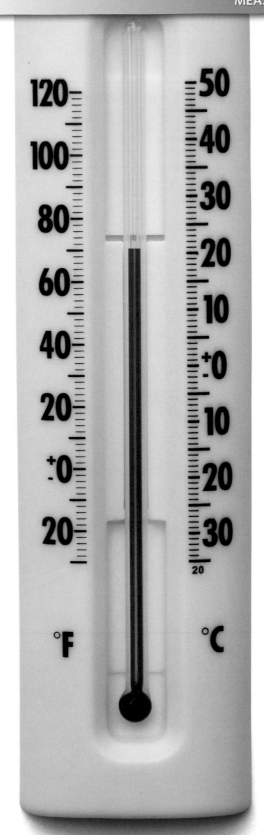

CHAPTER FOUR

HOW THERMOMETERS WORK

TYPES OF THERMOMETER

A liquid-in-glass thermometer relates temperature to the movement of a column of liquid expanding in a narrow glass tube. A thermocouple thermometer uses the fact that two junctions between different metals held at different temperatures produce an electric voltage. In a platinum resistance thermometer temperature is measured in terms of the electrical resistance of a platinum wire coil. A digital thermometer gives a direct reading of temperature.

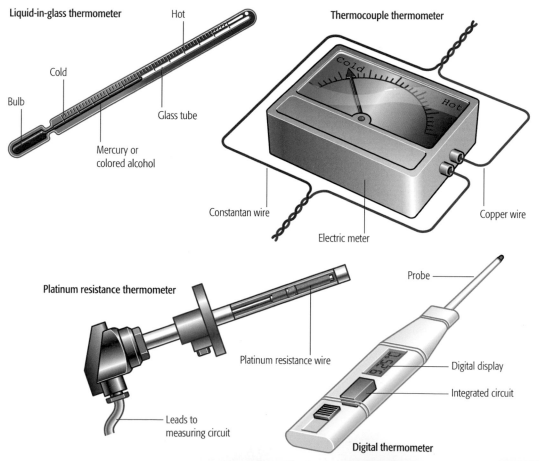

Liquid-in-glass thermometer

Hot

Cold

Bulb

Glass tube

Mercury or colored alcohol

Thermocouple thermometer

Cold

Hot

Constantan wire

Electric meter

Copper wire

Platinum resistance thermometer

Platinum resistance wire

Leads to measuring circuit

Probe

Digital display

Integrated circuit

Digital thermometer

Temperatures are measured using a thermometer, which is a device that utilizes some property of a substance that changes when the substance is heated. For instance, the common liquid-in-glass thermometer makes use of the fact that a liquid expands when heated. Another type makes use of the expansion of a metal when it is heated.

To express an object's level of hotness, we need a temperature scale (see page 15) and also a temperature-measuring device—a thermometer. The familiar mercury thermometer is a long, narrow glass tube with a bulb at one end that contains mercury. The other end of the tube is sealed. When the bulb is heated (by being placed where the temperature is to be measured), the mercury inside it expands and so moves along the tube. The distance it moves gives a measure of the temperature. The tube is graduated in degrees, either in Fahrenheit or Celsius.

A clinical thermometer is a special type used for taking a person's temperature. It works over only a narrow range, usually 35–42°C (95–108°F). A person's "normal" body temperature is 37°C (98.6°F). There is a narrow kink in the tube situated just above the bulb, so that when the thermometer is removed from the person's mouth, the mercury thread in the tube breaks at the kink. This leaves the upper end of the thread in position, so that the thermometer can be read. The mercury thread has to be shaken back into the bulb before the thermometer is used again.

Because mercury freezes into a solid at a temperature of –38.9°C (–38°F), a mercury thermometer cannot be used below this temperature. But alcohol does not freeze until the temperate drops to –117.3°C (–179°F), and so it is suitable for low-temperature thermometers. Alcohol

Today, doctors often take patients' temperatures with digital thermometers that give quick and accurate results.

is colorless, and it is dyed, usually red or blue, to make it show up.

USING METALS

The liquid-in-glass thermometers just described make use of the expansion of liquids when they are heated. Metals also expand slightly when heated, but it is difficult to make a mechanism that responds to the slight movement that results. The answer is to use two different metals, bonded together to form what is called a bimetallic strip. Steel and brass are often used because their expansions are very different. When a steel/brass bimetallic strip is heated, the brass expands more than the steel. This has the effect of making the strip bend, and such movement is made use of in some thermostats, which

are devices that maintain a constant temperature by controlling the flow of fuel or electricity to a heater.

In a thermometer based on this principle the bimetallic strip is a spiral that is fixed at one end. When the strip is heated, the spiral unwinds slightly. The movement is sufficient to move a pointer across a scale calibrated in degrees.

USING ELECTRICITY

In theory, any physical property that alters with a change in temperature can be used to make a thermometer. For example, in a thermocouple thermometer a junction between a pair of wires made from different metals is kept at a different temperature from another similar junction. This produces a small electric

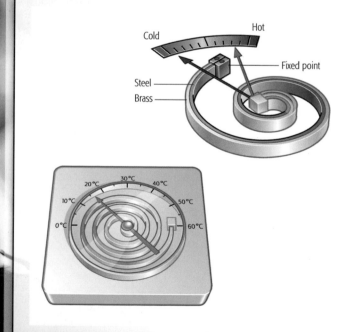

TWO-METAL SPIRAL

In this thermometer strips of steel and brass are bonded together to form a bimetallic strip. The strip is wound into a coil and fixed at one end. As the temperature rises, the brass expands more than the steel, and the strip uncoils slightly. This movement makes a pointer move around a temperature scale.

voltage in the wires. The voltage is measured with a sensitive voltmeter calibrated directly in degrees to give a measure of temperature.

Another electrical type is the platinum resistance thermometer. It contains a circuit that measures the change in electrical resistance of a platinum wire as its temperature changes. The resistance can then be matched to the actual temperature.

MAXIMUM AND MINIMUM

This type of thermometer, used in keeping weather records, shows the highest and lowest temperatures over a period. As the temperature rises, the alcohol in the right-hand bulb expands and the mercury rises in the left-hand tube. The mercury pushes a sprung steel marker, which stays in place when the temperature falls and the alcohol contracts. The mercury then rises in the right-hand tube, pushing a second marker. In this way the markers indicate the maximum and minimum temperatures.

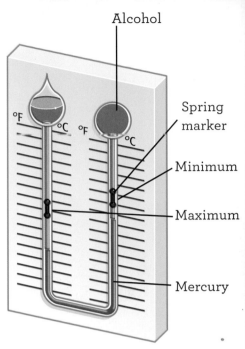

Alcohol

Spring marker

Minimum

Maximum

Mercury

CONVERTING SCALES

It is sometimes necessary to convert Celsius temperatures to Fahrenheit ones, or the other way around—Fahrenheit to Celsius. This involves a little simple math. To change Celsius to Fahrenheit, multiply by 9 and divide by 5 (or just multiply once by 1.8), then add 32. For example, to convert 50°C to Fahrenheit:

$$\frac{50 \times 9 = 90,}{5} \qquad 90 + 32 = 122°F$$

To convert Fahrenheit to Celsius, we reverse the procedure. First subtract 32, then multiply the result by 5, and divide by 9 (or just multiply once by 0.56). For example, to convert 86°F to Celsius:

$$86 - 32 = 54, \qquad \frac{54 \times 5}{9} = 30°C$$

Conversion of Celsius to Kelvin is easy—just add 273. For Kelvin to Celsius, subtract 273. Conversion of Fahrenheit to Kelvin is a nuisance. You first have to convert from Fahrenheit to Celsius and then add 273. Reverse the process for converting Kelvin to Fahrenheit.

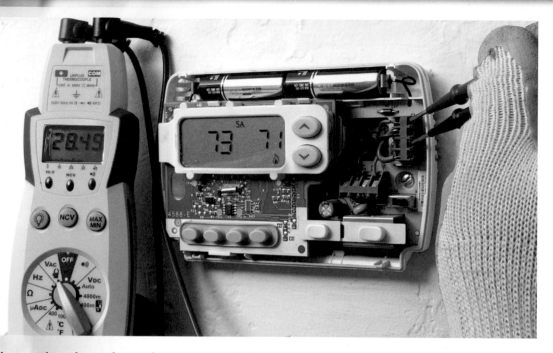

Above: This photo shows the inner panel of an electric thermostat. Right: Meteorologists must keep accurate records of temperatures around the world.

HIGH TEMPERATURES

Very high temperatures, such as those in a furnace, are measured using a pyrometer. In this type the electric current flowing through a wire filament is adjusted until it has the same brightness as the furnace as viewed through the eyepiece. The meter measures the current, but is marked in degrees.

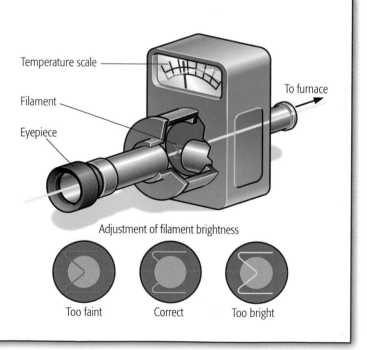

Temperature scale

Filament

Eyepiece

To furnace

Adjustment of filament brightness

Too faint   Correct   Too bright

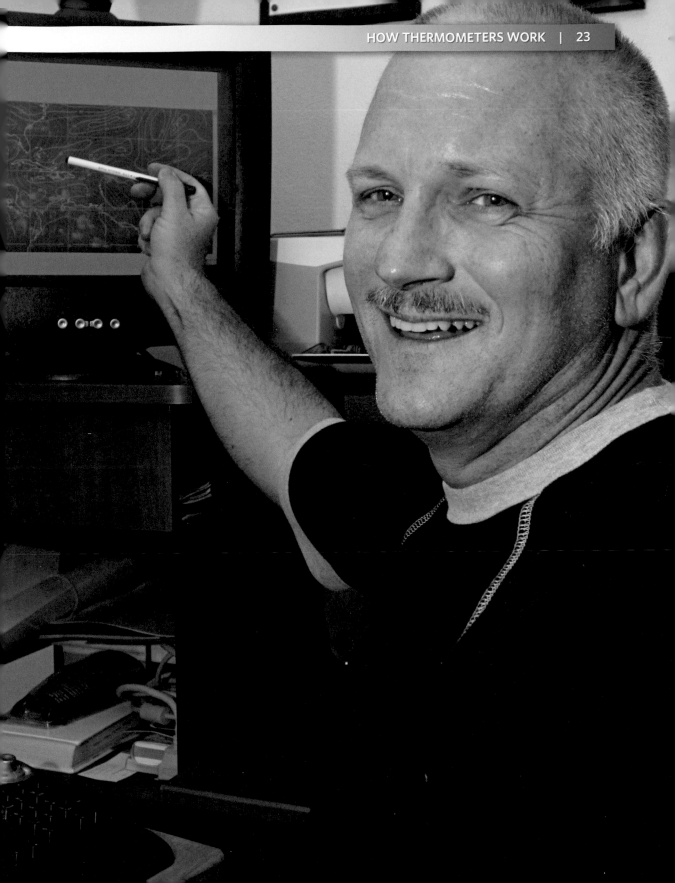

CHAPTER FIVE

REACTING TO HEAT

It takes nearly twice as much heat energy to raise the temperature of a cup of water by 10 degrees as it does to raise the temperature of a cup of alcohol by the same amount. That is because water has a higher specific heat capacity than alcohol. Different metals also have different specific heat capacities.

How substances react to the addition of heat depends on what they are. All get hotter, but some warm up more readily than others. The amount of heat needed to raise the temperature of an object by 1 degree Kelvin (see page 15) is called its heat capacity, measured in joules per kelvin (J/K). The amount of heat needed to raise the temperature of

SPECIFIC HEAT CAPACITIES

Different amounts of heat, expressed in joules, are needed to raise the temperatures of one kilogram of various substances through 10 K. The amounts vary because of the different specific heat capacities of the substances. Water has the highest specific heat capacity of any liquid, and aluminum has the highest among the common metals.

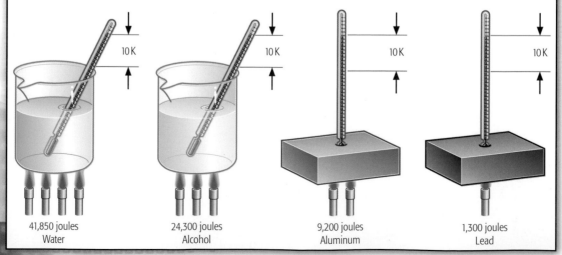

41,850 joules
Water

24,300 joules
Alcohol

9,200 joules
Aluminum

1,300 joules
Lead

Heat and Temperature

This illustration shows what happens when the same amount of heat (in this case 1 kilojoule, or 1,000 joules) is supplied to the same amounts of different substances. The temperature of water rises by only 1 K (1.8°F), while that of gold goes up by 32 K (57.6°F). The specific heat capacities are also shown.

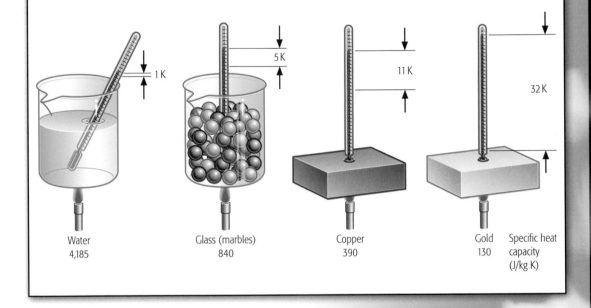

| Water | Glass (marbles) | Copper | Gold | Specific heat |
| 4,185 | 840 | 390 | 130 | capacity (J/kg K) |

1 kilogram of a substance by 1 K is called its specific heat capacity, which is measured in the more complicated units of joules per kilogram per degree kelvin (J/kg K). Specific heat capacity can also be expressed using kilocalories, in units of kcal/kg K. The specific heat capacity of water is 4,185 J/kg K (equivalent to 1 kcal/kg K), which is the highest of any known substance. It is twice as large as that of ice and over 32 times that of gold. Most metals have low specific heat capacities.

STORE AND RELEASE

One way of getting warm is to heat an object and then let it slowly release its heat. This is the principle of the hot-water bottle. The hot water inside the bottle stores heat, which is slowly released into the bed. Water's high specific heat capacity makes it ideal for this purpose.

But you cannot heat a room with hot-water bottles! You could use a block of concrete, which has the highest heat capacity of common solids. Called a

storage heater, the block is electrically heated (often using cheap electricity available at night) and then allowed to release its heat to keep the room warm the next day.

Left: The joule, a unit of measurement, is named for James Joule. Right: Hot water bottles are often used to soothe sore muscles.

JAMES JOULE

James Joule (1818–1889) was a British physicist best known for establishing the connections between electricity and heat and between mechanical energy and heat. In 1840 he announced what is now called Joule's law, which relates the electricity flowing in a wire and the wire's resistance to the amount of heat produced. Three years later he worked out how much heat is produced by a given amount of mechanical work, by measuring the heat produced when a container of water was stirred by paddles driven by falling weights. For several years Joule worked with William Thomson (Lord Kelvin), and between them they discovered the Joule–Thomson effect, in which a gas is cooled when it escapes through narrow holes. The effect is the basic principle of the refrigerator.

CHAPTER SIX

CHANGING STATES

It takes a certain amount of heat to raise the temperature of water to its boiling point. But you have to keep on supplying heat to boiling water to convert it into steam. This extra heat is called latent heat. Latent heat is also needed to change ice into water.

Whenever a solid melts to form a liquid, or a liquid boils to form a gas or vapor, we say that a change of state occurs. Similar changes happen when a gas or vapor condenses to form a liquid, or when a liquid freezes to form a solid.

Every change of state involves the absorption or release of heat. It takes

Water can be enjoyed in its solid form as snow.

heat to melt ice—not just to raise its temperature but to change it from a solid to a liquid. This heat is called latent heat, and for ice it takes 80 kcal to melt 1 kg. Its temperature remains at 0°C—freezing point—all the time. (This is one area where kilocalories are generally used instead of joules for measuring heat.) Thus we say that the latent heat of fusion of ice is 80 kcal/kg. Not surprisingly, the latent heat of freezing of water is exactly the same.

You have to remove 80 kcal from 1 kg of water in order to convert it into ice.

The latent heat of vaporization applies to the other change of state, from liquid to gas or vapor. For water it has a value of 540 kcal/kg: It takes 540 kcal to change 1 kg of liquid water at 100°C into 1 kg of steam at the same temperature. The latent heat of condensation, the amount of heat that must be removed to convert 1 kg of steam at 100°C to 1 kg of liquid water at 100°C, is also 540 kcal.

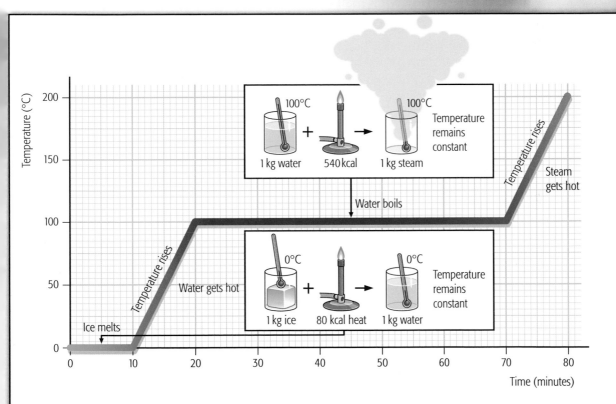

HIDDEN HEAT

The word "latent" means "hidden," and this diagram shows where the hidden heat goes. First, it takes 80 kcal (80,000 calories) to melt 1 kg of ice supplied with heat at the rate of 10 kilocalories per minute. Then, when the water has been heated to its boiling point, it takes another 540 kcal to turn 1 kg of water into 1 kg of steam.

When a liquid evaporates it takes heat from its surroundings. That is why sweating makes you cooler. The latent heat of vaporization of the watery sweat is removed from your skin.

SUBLIMATION

A few solids are unusual because when they are heated they turn directly into a vapor without melting first. This process is given the name sublimation, and the solid is said to sublime. It occurs because the boiling point of the solid is actually less than its melting point at atmospheric pressure. Examples of substances that sublime are solid carbon dioxide ("dry ice") and iodine. At any temperature above –78.5°C (about –109°F) solid carbon dioxide changes directly into a gas.

Carbon dioxide and iodine sublime at ordinary atmospheric pressure. Other solids can be made to sublime by greatly reducing the pressure on them. This is the principle of the freeze-drying process for foods and instant coffee. The food is frozen at very low pressure so that the ice sublimes out of it to leave behind a dehydrated product. Conversely, at high pressures a substance that sublimes at atmospheric pressure can be made to melt in the usual way. Liquid carbon dioxide can be produced at high pressures.

HEAT OF VAPORIZATION

Once the water in a kettle is boiling, supplying more heat turns the boiling water into steam. This latent heat of vaporization, as it is called, equals 540 kcal per kilogram for water (about 511 kcal per quart). Most liquids have much lower latent heats of vaporization. For example, for alcohol it is 204 kcal per kg, and for mercury it is only 71 kcal per kg.

Handling dry ice, seen here, without protection can cause burns from frostbite on a person's skin.

CHAPTER SEVEN

FLUID AND GAS EXPANSION

To a physicist a fluid is any gas or liquid, such as air, steam, or water. These two states of matter are grouped together because they share a common property: They can both flow—hence the name. Fluids also share another property: They expand when they are heated. This property is employed in thermometers of various kinds.

The expansion of hot gases is what drives a shell out of a gun, demonstrated here by a World War II battleship preparing to fire several shots at once.

EXPANSION OF MERCURY

A teaspoonful of mercury equals about 5 ml (milliliters), which is the volume of mercury in a large laboratory thermometer. The illustration shows how much this volume of mercury expands when heated to 50°C and to 100°C.

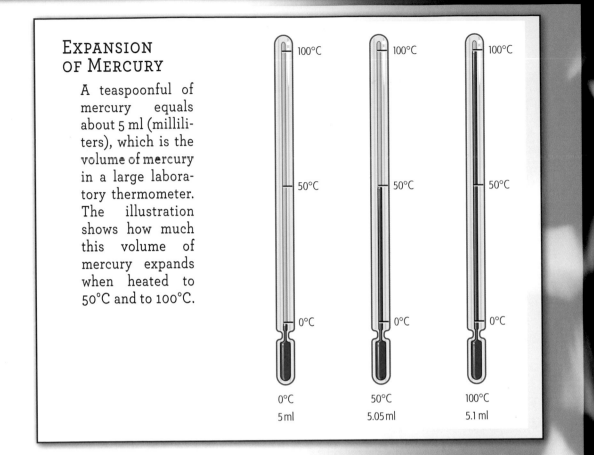

0°C	50°C	100°C
5 ml	5.05 ml	5.1 ml

On previous pages we looked at the expansion of liquids several times. We have seen, for example, how a liquid-in-glass thermometer works (see page 19 and the illustration above). A liquid or gas has no definite shape—it takes up the shape of the vessel containing it. For these, we can therefore consider only volume expansion. (Of course, making a liquid expand along a narrow tube, as in a thermometer, has the effect of producing what appears to be linear expansion—along a line.)

For a liquid, expansion is measured as its coefficient of volume expansion (also called volume expansivity). This is the proportion by which the original volume expands when the temperature is increased by 1 K. These coefficients are very small, but still up to ten times larger than those for solids, and they vary slightly depending on the temperature at which they are measured. For example, water has a coefficient of volume expansion of 0.0003 per K, while that of mercury is even smaller at 0.000018

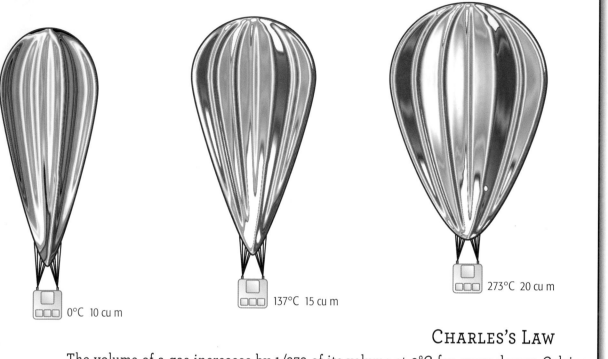

0°C 10 cu m

137°C 15 cu m

273°C 20 cu m

CHARLES'S LAW

The volume of a gas increases by 1/273 of its volume at 0°C for every degree Celsius rise in temperature. Therefore a ballon with a volume of 10 cu m (cubic meters) at 0°C increases in volume to 15 cu m at 137°C and doubles in volume to 20 cu m at 273°C.

per K. Mathematically the coefficient is equal to the increase in volume divided by the original volume per degree K rise in temperature.

ABSOLUTE OR APPARENT?

It is straightforward to define the coefficient of volume expansion of a liquid—we have just done so. But it is quite another matter to try to measure it. That is because the liquid has to be held in a container of some sort, and any attempt to measure its expansion on heating has to take into account the fact that the container will expand as well.

This difficulty can be demonstrated by making a mark on the side of a glass beaker level with the surface of a liquid. When the beaker is heated (from below), the level of the liquid falls at first as the beaker expands. Then, as the heat reaches the liquid, it too expands, and its level rises above the mark. As a result we can only measure the apparent expansion of the liquid. For this reason physicists sometimes distinguish between a liquid's absolute (or true) coefficient of expansion and its apparent coefficient of expansion. There are ways of getting around this difficulty if we know the coefficient of volume expansion of the material of the beaker, in this case glass.

WATER'S DENSITY

In the same way that ice is a very unusual solid because it expands as it cools, water is also exceptional in the way that it behaves. When cold water is warmed from a temperature of 0°C to 4°C, it takes up less volume—it contracts. Above 4°C it begins to expand, behaving in the same way as most other liquids.

Also, because density equals mass divided by volume, and warming does not change the mass of water, water must be at its densest at about 4°C. This effect has extremely important consequences for fish. Since water near the surface of a lake cools toward the freezing point in winter, its density increases, and it sinks to the bottom. Eventually the surface water reaches a temperature of 4°C; but then, as it cools further, the colder water stays at the top—because it is less dense than the water lower down. Even when the surface freezes and forms ice, the water at the bottom stays liquid at 4°C and provides a safe home for fish.

VOLUME AND PRESSURE

Heating increases the volume of a gas as long as its pressure is kept the same. Like a liquid, a gas therefore has a coefficient of volume expansion defined as the increase in volume of 1 cu cm of a gas at 0°C for a rise in temperature of 1 K (at constant pressure). It turns out to have the same value for all gases and is equal to 0.00366 per degree K. This is

Ice fisherman often drill holes through the frozen ice of lakes to catch fish swimming below.

The giant balloons used in the Macy's Thanksgiving Day Parade are filled with a gas called helium.

equal to the fraction 1/273, as predicted by Charles's law. The law states that at constant pressure the volume of a given mass of gas increases by 1/273 of its volume at 0°C for every degree Kelvin rise in temperature. As a result, the volume of a gas at a constant pressure is proportional to its absolute temperature: that is, its temperature on the Kelvin temperature scale (remember that degrees Kelvin equals degrees Celsius plus 273).

Gases have another coefficient of expansion, which is measured in terms of changes in gas pressure when the volume is kept constant. It is called the pressure coefficient and turns out to be equal to 0.00366 per K (or 1/273 per K), the same as the volume coefficient. This fact should come as no surprise because both coefficients represent the effect of heating on the molecules.

At constant pressure the molecules acquire more energy and move farther apart and so increase the volume. At constant volume the more energetic molecules collide with the walls of the container more frequently and thus increase the pressure.

GASES IN ACTION

The pressure created by heating a gas can be made to do work. For example, gas pressure is used in steam engines, internal combustion engines (gasoline and diesel), gas turbines, and pneumatic tools. Hot expanding gases are also the propellants in rockets and guns. Balloons also contain gas. In a hot-air balloon air is heated so that it expands and becomes less dense than the surrounding air, making the balloon rise. Expansion caused by heating also has to be taken into account with gas-filled balloons, as explained on the opposite page.

This antique steam engine uses gas pressure to move through the countryside.

Heated expaning gases propell space shuttle Atlantis into outer space.

Each year hundreds of hot air balloons take part in the Albuquerque International Balloon Fiesta.

CHAPTER EIGHT

EXPANDING SOLIDS

When a solid is heated, the atoms or molecules of which it is composed vibrate more vigorously. Because these particles vibrate more, they take up more room. As a result the solid gets bigger—it expands. And the more you heat it, the larger it gets.

Expansion of solids—particularly metals—can be a nuisance. It can cause steel railroad lines to buckle and concrete roads to crack. In the Middle East high daytime temperatures cause oil pipelines to expand and lengthen, which would also result in buckling if the pipes did not include expansion loops. Even overhead power lines can droop dangerously low when the metal cables expand in summer.

But like most other phenomena in physics, the expansion of solids has also been put to good use. For example, the difference in expansion between two different metals bonded together in bimetallic devices has already been described, on page 20. Some other uses are illustrated on these pages, but first we should understand why expansion occurs.

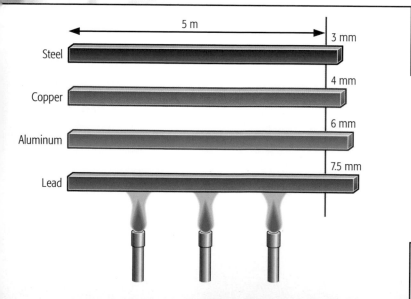

5 m

Steel — 3 mm

Copper — 4 mm

Aluminum — 6 mm

Lead — 7.5 mm

EXPANDING METALS

Different metals expand by different amounts when they are heated. The diagram shows the amount of expansion when 5-meter lengths are heated through 50°C (about 90°F).

MOLECULES IN MOTION

All solids are made up of atoms and molecules. These particles are in a constant state of motion—after all, their vibrations are what defines heat. Add more heat, and they vibrate more vigorously (and the temperature of the solid rises). One consequence of this extra molecular motion is that the solid expands. A long bridge may expand by a meter or more (3 feet or more) when it heats up in summer. The actual amount of expansion will depend on what the bridge is made of. Steel, for example, usually expands more than concrete.

LINEAR AND VOLUME EXPANSION

A scientific measure of how much a solid increases in length when heated is its coefficient of linear expansion (also called expansivity). It is defined as the proportion by which its original length increases when its temperature rises through 1 K. The coefficient of linear expansion is very small for most solids, varying from only 0.0000005 per K for the glassy substance quartz to 0.000024 per K for the metal lead. What these tiny figures mean in real terms is illustrated on the opposite page.

RAILROAD EXPANSION

Railroad rails are made of steel, which, like other metals, expands when heated. On light railroads, slotted bolt holes allow the rails to move in hot weather.

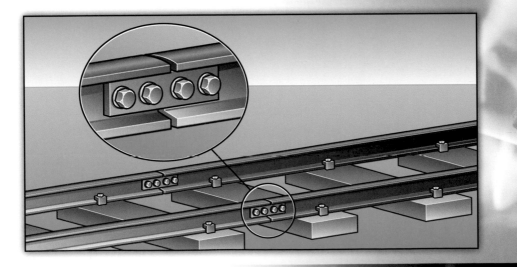

Pipelines carrying oil across long distances are built with expansion loops so they do not buckle when the metal of the pipe expands.

Heated solids also increase their volume, so they have in addition a coefficient of volume expansion (just like liquids and gases). Think of a cube. When it is heated, each of its three dimensions increases. It is therefore not surprising that the coefficient of volume expansion is usually three times the value of the coefficient of linear expansion.

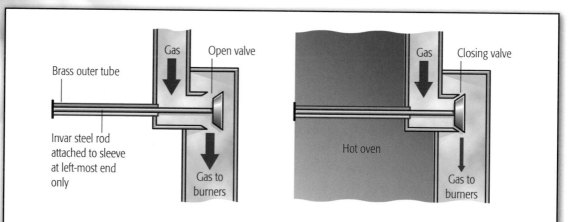

GAS CONTROL VALVE

When the valve is open, it admits gas to an oven's burners. As the oven heats up, a brass tube in the oven expands and lengthens. This action pulls a rod of Invar (an alloy that does not expand when heated) and closes the valve to reduce the gas flow.

The George Washington Bridge, constructed of steel, connects New York and New Jersey.

CHAPTER NINE

CONDUCTORS AND INSULATORS

The handle of a metal spoon left in a hot drink quickly warms up and may get too hot to hold. Heat travels along the spoon by conduction. But not all materials conduct heat as well as metals do.

Very poor conductors of heat are called insulators.

We all know that heat can travel easily through some substances, such as the metal spoon placed in the hot drink.

HOW HEAT TRAVELS

Heat travels through a solid by conduction. Imagine that the solid bar in this illustration has its lower end in a fire. The atoms at this hot end vibrate vigorously. These "hot" atoms joggle their neighbors, and they in turn joggle their neighbors, but not quite so much. The middle of the bar gets warm. Only at the cold end do the atoms vibrate normally. In a metal, heat is conducted mainly by free electrons moving between the atoms.

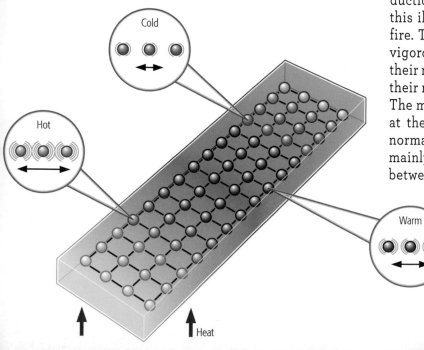

Cold

Hot

Warm

Heat

Other substances do not conduct heat very well—the handle of a plastic spoon hardly gets warm if the spoon is left in a hot drink. So how does heat travel in this way, and why are metals better heat conductors than plastics are?

As with many other phenomena in physics, to answer these questions we have to take a look at the atomic or molecular structure of the materials. A metal is made up of regularly spaced atoms that vibrate slightly around their normal positions. A "sea" of what are called free electrons occupies the spaces between the atoms.

When a substance is heated, its atoms vibrate more vigorously. The atoms at the hot end of a heated bar are the ones that vibrate the most. As they do so, they bump into their neighbors, increasing the neighbors' rate of vibration. Increased vibration means higher temperature. In this way the vibrations gradually increase along the length of the spoon, and this is how heat travels from the hot end toward the cool end. The atoms themselves do not move from their average positions. In a metal bar free electrons moving rapidly along it carry most of the heat.

The internal structure of a plastic spoon is quite different. Plastics are composed of large molecules with no free electrons between them. The molecules do vibrate, and a similar ripple effect does conduct some heat along the spoon. But the process is slow, and—more importantly—there are no free electrons to help.

We therefore say that metals are good conductors of heat, while nonmetals such as wood and plastics are poor conductors, or insulators. A saucepan is made of metal so that it will rapidly conduct heat from a stove to the pan's contents. But it has a wooden or plastic handle that does not get too hot for you to be able to pick up the pan.

You will find in another book of this series an explanation of how materials conduct electricity. There are good electrical conductors and there are poor electrical conductors, which are also known as insulators. As with heat, most of the good conductors of electricity are metals, while nonmetals make up most of the poor conductors. This similarity of behavior is no coincidence.

Both kinds of conduction depend to some extent on the same property of the material—the number of free electrons available in its structure. With electricity the free electrons carry current through the material. And with heat the "hot" free electrons have a high kinetic energy, which they carry through the material to the colder part before giving it up in collisions with atoms. Insulators—both electrical insulators and heat insulators—do not have free electrons to fulfill these functions.

RATE OF CONDUCTION

Several things affect the rate at which heat is conducted by a substance. Consider a block of material with one end being heated. The rate of heat flow through the block depends on its length. The longer it is, the more slowly heat flows from one end to the other. The cross-sectional area of the block also matters—the greater this area, the faster heat will flow. The difference in temperature between the two ends of the block is also obviously important. The greater this difference, the faster heat will flow.

Finally, there is a property of the material itself that is a measure of how well it conducts heat. It is the material's thermal conductivity. When heat is measured in joules, the units of thermal conductivity are watts per meter per K. The illustration on the opposite page compares the thermal conductivities of various substances. Silver is the best heat conductor of all, while the poorest are feathers and the vegetable fiber kapok. That is why these sorts of materials are used for heat insulation in bed covers and padded winter clothing.

Notice that cork is a particularly poor conductor. You can feel this for yourself if you compare walking in bare feet on a ceramic tiled floor and walking on a floor covered with cork tiles. Cork feels much warmer because it does not easily conduct the heat away from your feet. For a similar reason fiberglass, or glass wool, is used for insulating lofts and for wrapping water pipes to prevent them from freezing in winter.

Solid plastic foams, also called expanded plastics, are very poor heat conductors (or good heat insulators). A common example is expanded polystyrene, commonly known as Styrofoam. Notice how you can hold a Styrofoam cup containing a hot drink: That is because the plastic does not conduct the heat to your fingers. Foam plastics are sometimes inserted into the cavity walls of buildings. They are pumped in as liquids that soon solidify and form a layer of heat insulation. This makes the building cool in summer

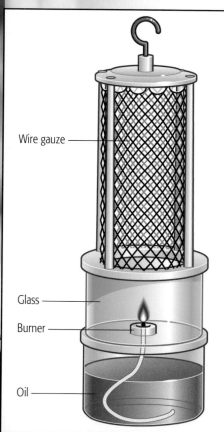

Wire gauze

Glass

Burner

Oil

SAFETY LAMP

The safety lamp was invented at a time when coal miners had only oil lamps to light their way underground. Sometimes, a dangerously flammable gas called fire-damp (methane) spread through mines and the oil lamps ignited it, causing disastrous explosions. The wire gauze in the safety lamp conducts the heat of the flame away from the gas outside, which does not therefore get hot enough to ignite.

(by keeping the Sun's heat out) and warm in winter (by stopping internal heat from escaping through the walls).

FLUIDS AND GASES

Heat can also travel through fluids—liquids and gases—by conduction, although this is not the usual way heat travels in such substances (see page 50–51). Air has a thermal conductivity of 0.025 watts per meter per K, which is about the same as the conductivity of feathers. This means that air is a very poor conductor or, put another way, a very good heat insulator. It explains why furs and loosely knitted clothing keep you warm in winter. The air trapped in the materials acts as an additional insulator.

GOOD AND BAD CONDUCTORS

These charts show the thermal conductivities of common materials (in watts per meter per degree K). You can see why feathers and kapok make good insulators to line padded clothing.

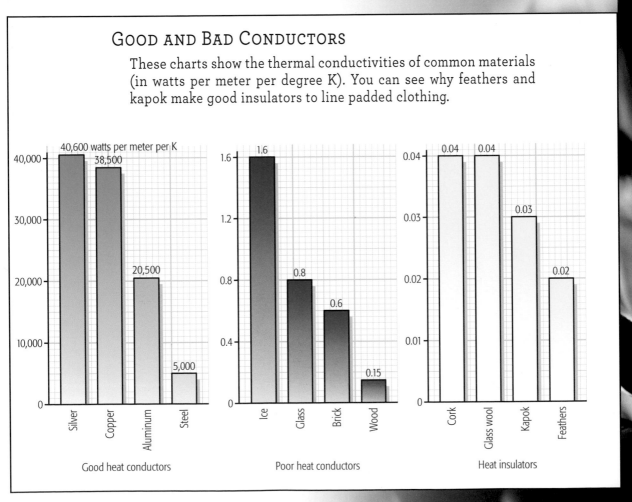

Good heat conductors

Poor heat conductors

Heat insulators

The temperature of a furnace has to be in excess of 900°C (about 1,650°F) to soften glass. The glassblower holds a rod made of a poor heat conductor so he does not burn his hands.

This woman keeps snug and warm in her fur-lined parka. Fur is a very poor conductor of heat and therefore a good insulator to keep out the cold.

CHAPTER TEN

CIRCULATING HEAT

Smoke from a fire always rises because the fire heats the air above it, which becomes less dense and goes upward. Surrounding cold air moves toward the fire, gets hotter, and also rises. This circulation of heat by a moving gas is called convection.

Heat normally travels through a fluid—a gas or a liquid—by convection. In this process the material itself

CLOUD FORMATION

Convection currents can cause clouds to form. Warm air, heated by the land, can hold more water vapor than cold air can. Convection makes this warm air rise, where the water vapor cools and condenses out as clouds of water droplets.

Warm air

THERMAL LIFT

Thermals are air currents that move upward over a warm part of the ground. As well as affecting the weather, thermals provide a free ride for soaring birds such as eagles. They generally gain height in a long, lazy spiral.

actually moves (which is why it cannot take place in solids). When a hot fluid moves, it takes heat with it and displaces any cold fluid in its way. Also, cold fluid moves in to take the place of the rising hot fluid. In this way the fluid circulates by creating a convection current.

The hot fluid is less dense than the cold fluid that surrounds it. As a result it is more buoyant and tends to rise, just like a helium balloon or a piece of wood floating on water. Such natural convection currents have various uses. Soaring birds such as albatross and eagles make use of updrafts of warm air, called thermals, and can fly for miles without wasting energy by flapping their wings. Pilots of gliders and hang gliders also make use of thermals to keep their aircraft flying without the use of motors. They know from experience that thermals occur over land that

has been heated by the Sun and seek them out in order to spiral upward and gain altitude.

WEATHER CURRENTS

Large-scale convection currents in the atmosphere play an important part in creating and controlling the weather. As the air near the ground becomes warmer, it retains water vapor because warm air can hold more moisture than cold air can. Eventually the warm air rises, rather like a thermal, carrying the water vapor with it. But when this air meets the colder air above, it can no longer hold all the water vapor, which condenses out as tiny droplets of water. These masses of droplets are clouds, in this case the type of cloud called cumulus (from the Latin word for "mass").

Convection currents also give rise to winds and breezes. Near a seacoast in summer, during the day the land warms up more quickly than the sea. The warm air above the land rises, cools, and then sinks down again over the sea. This sets up a circulating convection current with a gentle wind blowing onshore off the sea, called a sea breeze. The situation is reversed at night, because then the land cools down more rapidly than the sea. The result is a land breeze, blowing out to sea.

CONVECTION IN WATER

Warm water can also transfer heat by convection, and for the same reason. The warm water is less dense than surrounding colder water, and it rises, setting up a convection current. The principle is used in some hot-water heating systems in homes and offices (see the illustration on page 53). Hot water from a boiler rises and enters a cylindrical hot-water tank, where it transfers its heat to water circulating around the radiators.

On a much larger scale, convection takes place in the world's oceans. Water near the equator is warmer and less dense

CAR COOLING SYSTEM

The heat produced by burning gasoline or diesel fuel makes a car's engine very hot. It is cooled by circulating oil and by pumping water around spaces within the engine block. The water, heated by the engine, is cooled by the radiator, which is a type of heat exchanger in which cold air flows through its honeycomb structure.

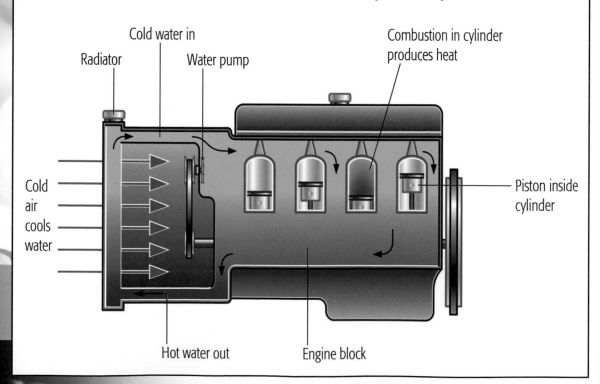

Radiator

Cold water in

Water pump

Combustion in cylinder produces heat

Cold air cools water

Piston inside cylinder

Hot water out

Engine block

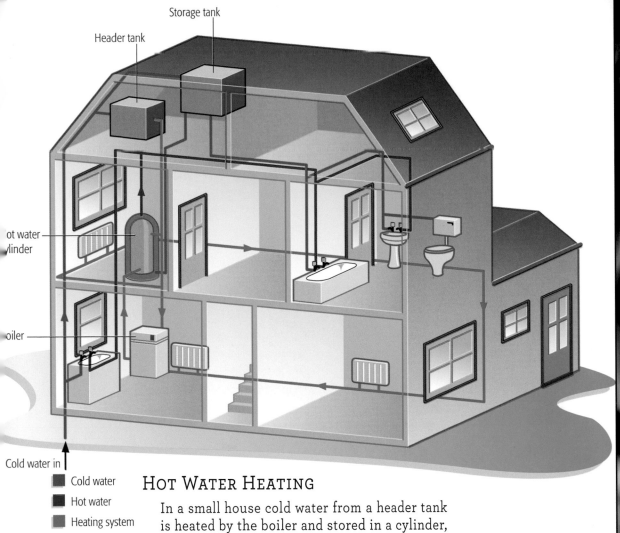

Storage tank

Header tank

ot water
linder

oiler

Cold water in

- ◼ Cold water
- ◼ Hot water
- ◼ Heating system

Hot Water Heating

In a small house cold water from a header tank is heated by the boiler and stored in a cylinder, from where it convects around the radiators.

than the water nearer the poles. It tends to stay close to the surface and is displaced by colder water from polar regions. The deep-water currents that result shift huge volumes of water. Between Greenland and Iceland, for example, 5 million cu m (1 billion gallons) of water flows into the North Atlantic every second. This type of flow should not be confused with currents like the Gulf Stream, which are a surface effect caused mainly by the wind.

MANMADE CONVECTION

Even when there are no density differences that will set up natural convection, blowers (for air) and pumps (for water) can circulate fluids to transfer heat. A hot-air heating system has fans to blow air heated by a furnace along ducts to each room. In a car's cooling system a pump circulates cooling water between the engine and the radiator.

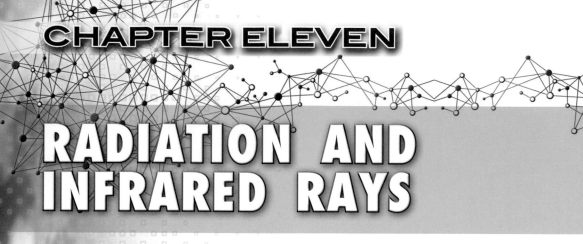

CHAPTER ELEVEN

RADIATION AND INFRARED RAYS

The heat of the Sun that we feel on our faces has traveled 150 million kilometers across the empty vacuum of space. Over a much shorter distance we can feel the heat of a fire if we hold our hands near it. This kind of heat transfer is called radiation. Heat that is transferred by radiation travels in the form of invisible infrared rays.

We have seen the way in which heat can travel through solid substances by conduction and through fluids by convection. We will now consider a method of heat transfer that needs no medium in which to travel—radiation.

A thermograph is a photograph that indicates temperatures by means of different colors. Yellow and red indicate hot, while blue and green indicate cold.

6

In radiation energy travels as electromagnetic waves. There are many kinds of these waves, including gamma rays, X-rays, microwaves, and radio waves. The most familiar are the waves of visible light—which enable us to see—and their invisible companions, ultraviolet light and infrared radiation. They all have different wavelengths, and they all travel at the speed of light. The waves that mainly concern us here, infrared radiation, possess wavelengths that are slightly longer than the wavelengths of visible light.

Any object whose temperature is above absolute zero gives off infrared radiation. In other words, every normal object emits some infrared. But the hotter the object, the more infrared it emits. You cannot see the radiation from a hot radiator in a room, but you can feel it if you carefully place your hand near the radiator. In fact, another name for infrared is heat radiation. All the heat radiated by the Sun is in the form of infrared.

SEEING RADIATION

Scientists use various instruments and techniques to detect electromagnetic radiation. Electronic circuits connected to an antenna can detect microwaves and radio waves.

Gamma rays, X-rays, and visible light can be detected by photographic film, as in a camera or an X-ray machine. Special film can also detect ultraviolet light and infrared radiation, while astronomers use various electronic devices to study such radiations that are emitted by heavenly bodies.

Alternatively, infrared radiation can be measured using a device called a thermograph. It produces a picture of a hot object, with the temperatures of various areas represented as different colors or shades of gray. Thermographs are used in medicine, for example, for diagnosing tumors. The skin over a tumor is slightly warmer than the skin around it and shows up as a light area on a thermograph. The thermograph on the opposite page shows the warmer and colder areas of a house.

THE COLOR OF HEAT

Infrared radiation comes from a hot object's vibrating atoms or molecules. The more they vibrate, the more radiation they emit. But increasing the vibration of an object's atoms also increases its temperature. It therefore follows that the amount of infrared radiation an object emits increases as its temperature rises.

The wavelength of the radiation also depends on the temperature of the emitting object. The higher the temperature (i.e., the greater the vibration), the shorter the wavelength. When an object is heated, it begins to emit more infrared. Then, as its gets hotter, it becomes red. At this stage its temperature is about 600–700°C (1,110–1,300°F). When it is even hotter, it turns orange (temperature 950°C/1,750°F), then yellow (temperature 1,100°C/2,000°F), and finally it becomes white hot at a temperature of about 1,400°C (2,550°F). It is now emitting white light as well as infrared radiation. In this way it is possible to estimate a hot object's temperature merely from its color, which is a skill used by blacksmiths and others who deal with very hot metals, and also by astronomers studying the stars.

Although infrared radiation is invisible to the human eye, scientists can make photographic film and television camera tubes that are sensitive to infrared. They have many practical uses. For example, infrared cameras on orbiting Earth satellites, such as the Landsat series, take infrared pictures of crops and other vegetation on which damaged or diseased plants show up differently than healthy ones.

CAPTURING ENERGY FROM THE SUN

Our largest source of radiant energy— mainly light and infrared radiation—is without doubt the Sun. It lies at the great distance of 150 million km (93 million miles) from Earth, and it emits radiation in all directions across the vacuum of interplanetary space. On the daylight side of the Earth radiant energy from the Sun arrives at a rate of 1.4 kilowatts per square meter (kW per m²). One way of capturing some of this free energy is to use a large, curved mirror to focus the Sun's radiation in a solar furnace. This radiation can also make electricity in solar cells, although they are expensive and not very efficient converters of energy. They tend to be reserved for spacecraft, where they last much longer than any battery would.

ELECTROMAGNETIC SPECTRUM

Visible light forms only a tiny part of the electromagnetic spectrum—the part that our senses can detect. We can also feel heat radiation from the infrared region of the spectrum. Longer wavelengths are microwaves and radio waves, which can also be used for heating. Shorter wavelengths, such as X-rays and gamma rays, have extremely high energies.

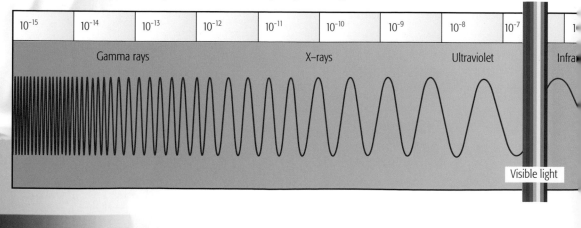

THREE WAYS THAT HEAT TRAVELS

If you put a metal rod in a pan of hot water, heat travels up the rod by conduction. Convection makes currents of water circulate from the heated bottom of the pan, and heat also escapes from the electric stove by means of radiation. These are the three ways that heat can travel.

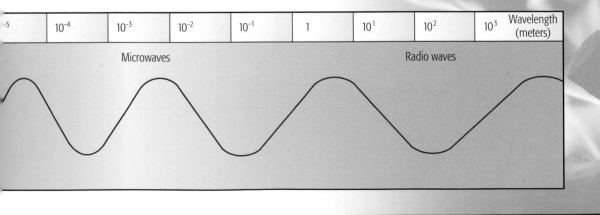

Conduction

Radiation

Convection

	10^{-4}	10^{-3}	10^{-2}	10^{-1}	1	10^1	10^2	10^3	Wavelength (meters)

Microwaves   Radio waves

CHAPTER TWELVE

TRAPPING AND EMITTING RADIATION

Everything emits some radiation, as explained in the previous chapter. Some things are better than others at emitting heat radiation. In general, black surfaces are good emitters—much better than surfaces that are white or shiny. That is why a hot drink will stay *hot longer in a shiny metal mug than in a dark-colored china cup.*

In addition, good emitters are good absorbers of heat radiation. The best absorber of all is a theoretical object called a black body, which absorbs all radiation falling on it. It is also the best

The tremendous heat produced by the Sun, shown here in an X-ray photograph, travels across space as infrared radiation. You can feel the loss of this heat when the Sun goes behind a cloud.

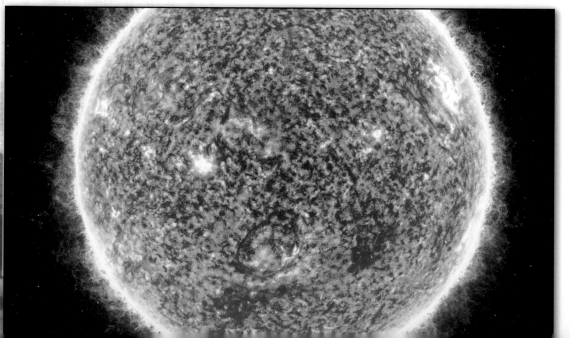

VACUUM BOTTLE

The vacuum bottle, or Dewar flask, is designed to prevent the loss of heat by all the processes described in the illustration on page 57. The vacuum prevents heat loss by conduction or convection, and the silver mirror minimizes loss through radiation. The stopper prevents heat loss through evaporation.

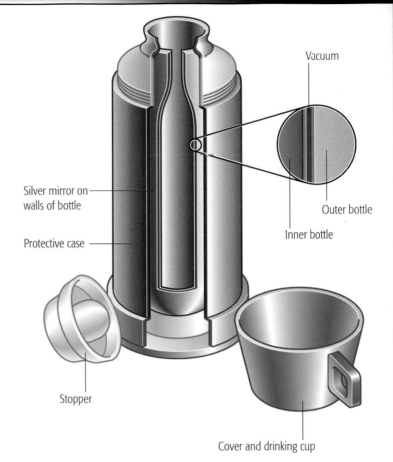

Silver mirror on walls of bottle

Protective case

Stopper

Vacuum

Outer bottle

Inner bottle

Cover and drinking cup

emitter. Nobody has been able to make a perfect black body, but a matte black surface comes very close to perfection. For this reason, a car's radiator is generally painted matte black so that it emits the heat from the water circulating inside it. Solar panels on houses are thin tanks containing water. They are also painted matte black, but this time in order to absorb as much of the Sun's heat radiation as possible to heat the water, which is then pumped into the house.

DEWAR FLASKS

A common need, both in science and in everyday life, is to prevent hot liquids from cooling down or cold liquids from warming up. The second of these problems faced the Scottish scientist James Dewar when he was dealing with liquid gases such as liquid nitrogen, which boils at −195.8°C (−352.4°F). His solution was the Dewar flask, or vacuum bottle, which we still use today, although mostly for keeping hot drinks hot.

The vacuum bottle (also called a thermos bottle) works because it prevents the three methods of heat transfer—conduction, convection, and radiation. It consists of two thin-walled glass bottles, one inside the other, with all the air removed from the space between them. This vacuum prevents heat from traveling by conduction because there is nothing for the heat to travel in. It also prevents heat from being transferred by convection because there is no fluid to circulate and carry the heat.

In addition, the glass walls of the double bottle are covered with a layer of silver, like a mirror. This silvered surface minimizes heat loss by radiation because shiny objects are very poor emitters of radiant heat.

ABSORBING AND EMITTING

When an object absorbs heat radiation, it becomes hotter than its surroundings. But any object that is hotter than its surroundings gives off heat. The heat emitted has a longer wavelength than the heat absorbed. This fact is put to good effect in a greenhouse, which traps heat.

The soil and plants inside a greenhouse absorb radiation from the sunlight that passes through the glass, making them warmer. They then reradiate the heat as longer-wavelength infrared radiation. But these longer waves cannot pass through glass, and as a result the heat is trapped inside the greenhouse. The temperature inside is up to 15–20 K (27–36°F) warmer than the outside.

JAMES DEWAR

James Dewar (1842–1923) was a Scottish chemist and physicist who lived and worked mainly in London. He is best known for inventing the vacuum bottle, or Dewar flask, in the early 1870s. He used his flasks during his researches into cryogenics (low temperatures), and by the year 1899 he had developed a large-scale method for liquefying hydrogen at a temperature of –253°C (–423°F). A year later he produced solid hydrogen at –259°C (–434°F). In chemistry, in 1889 with Frederick Abel he invented the propellant explosive cordite (based on guncotton), the first so-called smokeless powder. He also worked on specific heat capacities and on using the spectra of metallic elements as a means of identifying them. In 1904 he was knighted by King Edward VII.

GLOBAL WARMING

When fuels such as wood, coal, and oil burn, the carbon in them changes into carbon dioxide. This gas is also produced when gasoline or diesel fuel is burned in the engines of cars and trucks.

All this carbon dioxide passes into the air, where it forms a layer in the upper atmosphere. The incoming radiation from the Sun can penetrate the layer and pass through to warm the surface of the Earth. The surface then re emits radia tion as long-wave infrared, which cannot pass through the carbon dioxide layer. It is reflected back toward the Earth's surface, trapping the heat in the same way that a greenhouse does. This is called the greenhouse effect, and some scientists think that it may be responsible for global warming.

GREENHOUSE EFFECT

Much of the radiation from the Sun bounces off the Earth back into space. But some is absorbed and reemitted at longer wavelengths, then reflected back down by layers of carbon dioxide and other "greenhouse gases" in the atmosphere. As a result, the Earth's temperature may be slowly rising.

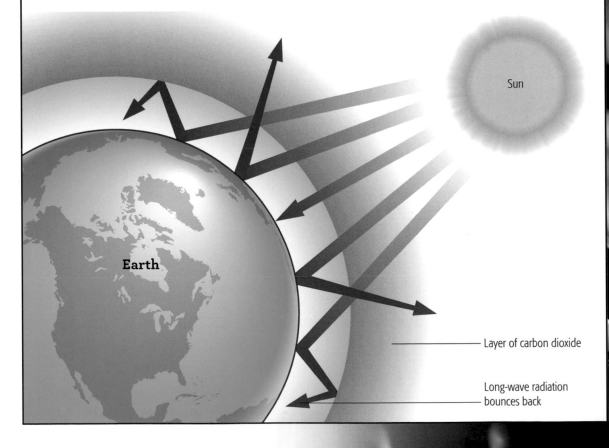

Sun

Earth

Layer of carbon dioxide

Long-wave radiation bounces back

Many Arab women (below) and children wear black robes in the heat of the desert sun. Although black absorbs heat, it is also a very good emitter of radiation and helps keep people, such as the man seen to the right, cool as they work.

CHAPTER THIRTEEN

FROM HOT TO COLD

We are used to making things warmer by supplying them with heat. But to make things colder, we have to remove heat from them.

The invention of the refrigerator to keep food cold had to wait for the discovery of some unusual physical effects.

All snowflake crystals are based on a six-sided, or hexagonal, form. The crystals grow when water vapor condenses in freezing clouds.

When you place your hand in a stream of air escaping through the valve of a bicycle tire, the air feels cold. Or when you spray your skin with an aerosol product, the skin feels extremely cold. In both cases high-pressure air or vapor has passed through a small hole or jet to a region of lower pressure.

This cooling effect is known as the Joule–Thomson effect after its two discoverers, James Joule and William Thomson, who later became Lord Kelvin (and so it is also sometimes called the Joule–Kelvin effect). It arises because work has to be done in order to separate the gas molecules, and the energy to do this is in the form of heat that is removed from the gas.

Energy in the form of heat also has to be supplied to turn a liquid into a vapor, and this energy is called the latent heat of vaporization (see chapter six). If a liquid is left to evaporate, it takes this heat from its surroundings, which therefore become cooler. A modern refrigerator makes use of both of these cooling effects.

INSIDE REFRIGERATORS

The key to a refrigerator is a liquid called freon, which boils at the very low temperature of about –30°C (–22°F). Cooling occurs when freon vapor passes through an expansion valve and is then allowed to evaporate. As it passes through the expansion valve, the temperature of the freon drops from about 38°C (100.4°F) to –8°C (–18.6°F), and in a section called the evaporator its temperature rises again to about 16°C (60.8°F). The freon absorbs heat while it evaporates.

The tubing that contains the evaporating freon coils around inside the ice-making compartment of the refrigerator, which is the coldest part. From the evaporator the freon vapor is sent on to a compressor, which "squeezes" the vapor and passes it to a condenser, where it gives off heat as it turns back into a liquid. For this reason the condenser is located on the outside of the refrigerator, where the heat evolved is lost to the surroundings.

In this way a refrigerator can be regarded as a heat engine working in reverse. Instead of supplying heat to do mechanical work, as in a heat engine, mechanical work (by the compressor) removes heat. The compressor, in turn, is powered by electricity, and this outside energy is used to make heat flow in the opposite way from normal, in this case from a cold region to a warmer region.

A heat pump uses similar principles to warm homes in winter and cool them in summer. In winter it acts as a space heater by removing heat from the air outside and passing it to the inside of the building. In summer it acts as air conditioning and removes heat from inside the building and passes it to the air outside.

Freons used in refrigerators are organic chemicals containing chlorine and fluorine atoms. They are examples of substances that are known as chlorofluorocarbons (CFCs). Their use is being phased out because freons from scrapped refrigerators enter the atmosphere, where they rise and can damage the ozone layer, which protects us from ultraviolet radiation given out by the Sun.

HOW A RERFRIGERATOR WORKS

A refrigerator removes heat from its contents. Its main components are shown in the illustration at the right. An ice-cold liquid called a refrigerant, such as freon, absorbs the heat and is thereby changed into a gas when it moves through an evaporator (inside the freezer compartment). There it removes heat from the freezer and gets slightly warmer. The gas is then squeezed by a compressor. The pressure turns it back into a liquid in the condenser loops. Heat produced by this process escapes to the outside air from the condenser loops. The continuous cycle of events is shown in the diagram below.

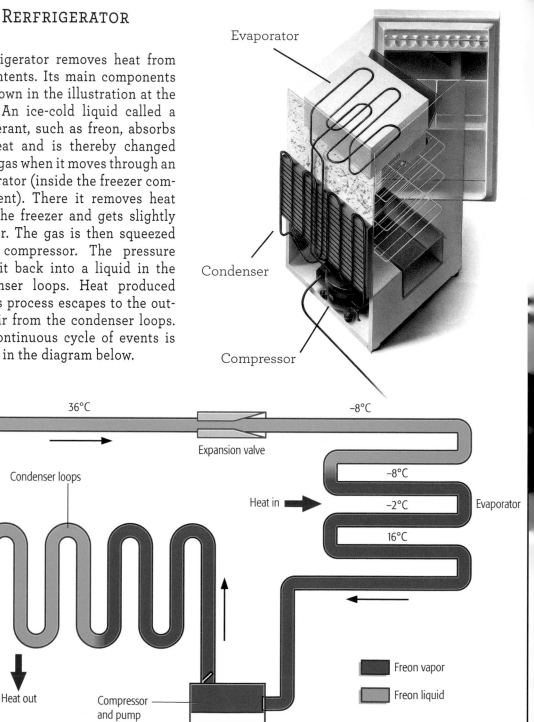

Evaporator

Condenser

Compressor

36°C

−8°C

Expansion valve

Condenser loops

Heat in

−8°C

−2°C

16°C

Evaporator

Heat out

Compressor and pump

Freon vapor

Freon liquid

LIQUEFYING GASES

If the pressure on a gas is made high enough, and as long as the gas is below its critical temperature, it turns to a liquid. The critical temperature is the temperature above which a gas cannot be liquefied by pressure alone. If the gas is above its critical temperature, it has to be cooled as well to liquefy it. For these reasons the production of liquid gases uses complicated high-pressure refrigeration.

Liquid air is the most commonly employed liquid gas. It has various uses in research and industry and is used as a source of other liquid gases—nitrogen, oxygen, argon, helium, neon, krypton, and xenon—which all occur in air. In the Linde process, invented by the German engineer Karl von Linde in 1895, air is alternately compressed, cooled, and expanded over and over. The temperature falls rapidly at each expansion stage because of the Joule-Thomson effect.

Keeping a refrigerator door open lets cold air escape. The refrigerator must then use more energy to keep its inner temperature constant.

LIQUID GASES

Air is a mixture of gases. Some of them occur in only trace amounts, but have important uses. They are separated out by first liquefying air and then letting it gradually warm up. The apparatus for doing this is a complex refrigerator.

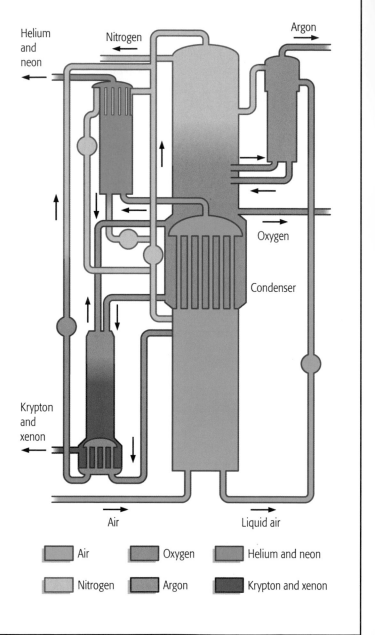

Helium and neon

Nitrogen

Argon

Oxygen

Condenser

Krypton and xenon

Air

Liquid air

| Air | Oxygen | Helium and neon |
| Nitrogen | Argon | Krypton and xenon |

EXPERIMENTING WITH COLD

The science of extremely low temperatures is called cryogenics. Scientists working in this area have for a long time tried to reach the temperature of absolute zero (0 K, –273°C or –460°F), which is the lowest temperature possible. In 1996 physicists reached a temperature of only 280 trillionths of a degree above absolute zero.

Some substances have unusual physical properties at such low temperatures. Some metals, for example, lose all

These laboratory samples are being kept cold in a cryogenic nitrogen container.

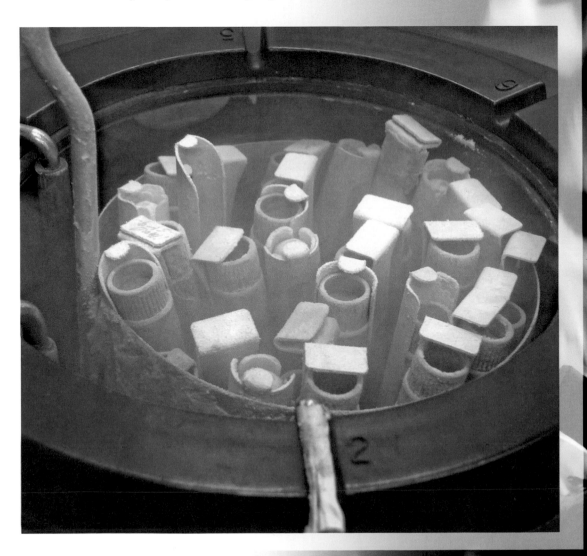

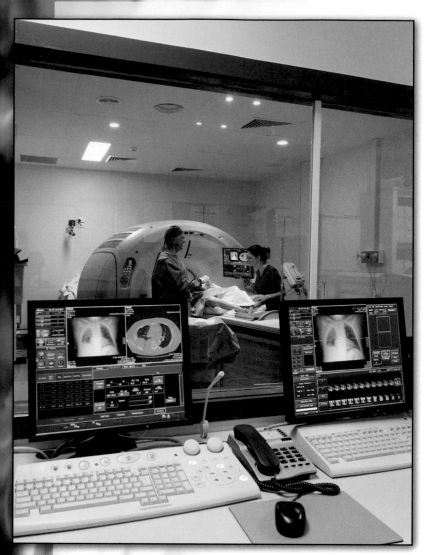

Superconducting magnets are used in Magnetic Resonance Imaging, or MRI, machines. The machines create images of what is going on inside a person's body, allowing doctors to make better diagnoses.

Superconductors can be made into very powerful electromagnets, which can theoretically be used for maglev (magnetic levitation) railroad trains. But such applications are still in the experimental stage mainly because it is very difficult to maintain the extremely low temperatures required for superconductivity.

Another strange low-temperature effect is called superfluidity. This term describes a fluid, such as liquid helium a few degrees above absolute zero, that flows without friction. Placed in a container, it flows vertically up the sides, over the lip, and escapes. On a slope it flows uphill against the force of gravity. So far scientists have found no practical uses for such superfluids.

their electrical resistance and become what are called superconductors. If a superconductor is made into an electrical circuit connected to a source of current, and the source is then removed, the current will continue to flow forever without stopping—some experimental superconducting circuits have continued to work for many years.

CHAPTER FOURTEEN

BIOGRAPHY: JAMES WATT

The first steam engine was built in 1712 by English inventor Thomas Newcomen (1663–1729), but the Scottish engineer James Watt refined the design to make it much more efficient and powerful. Watt's steam engine played a central role in the industrial revolution, which began in Britain in the early 1800s and later spread to continental Europe and the United States.

James Watt was born on January 19, 1736, in Greenock on the River Clyde in Scotland. His father was a carpenter by trade, but he also worked as a shipbuilder and general merchant.

The family was a wealthy one, but five of the Watt children had died in infancy. James was also found to be a delicate child, so it is not surprising that his parents were very protective of him in his early years. Watt was too sickly to attend school, so his mother tutored him at home. He had a bright and inquisitive mind from the start, and he would spend hours taking his toys apart and putting them back together again.

The work of James Watt contributed to the beginnings of the Industrial Revolution.

KEY DATES

1736	Born in Greenock, Scotland, on January 19
1755	Began apprenticeship as an instrument-maker in London
1764	Married his cousin, Margaret Miller
1769	Granted patent on separate condenser
1774	Moved to Birmingham and formed partnership with Matthew Boulton
1776	Married Ann MacGregor
1781	Patent granted on sun-and-planet gear wheel
1782	Designed double-acting rotary engine
1785	Made a fellow of the Royal Society, London
1819	Died at Heathfield Hall near Birmingham on August 25

When Watt did enter the local grammar school he failed to do very well, and it was not until the age of 13 that his ability began to emerge—this was when he was introduced to mathematics. At home in his father's workshop he spent any spare time building models. He also developed an interest in ships' instruments.

At the age of 17 Watt decided he wanted to become an instrument-maker, and in 1755 he traveled to London to become an apprentice: this meant he began learning the trade from someone already skilled in it. He returned to Scotland in 1757, where he set up a business in Glasgow making and repairing instruments of all kinds, including compasses and weighing scales. One of his duties was to make mathematical instruments for Glasgow University.

In 1764 Watt was asked to repair a model of a Newcomen engine. Watt had no difficulty in putting right the fault,

RICHARD TREVITHICK 1771–1833

A Cornishman, Trevithick grew up just at the time that Watt's steam engine was being introduced into the Cornish tin mines. He was barely literate but taught himself engineering, working initially on Watt's engines. An early convert to high-pressure engines, between 1801 and 1815 he built several steam road carriages, many stationary steam engines, and the world's first steam railway locomotive. He also invented the Cornish pumping engine, which soon replaced Watt's machines. In 1811, Trevithick was let down by a business partner and made bankrupt. Five years later he traveled to South America to deliver nine of his pumping engines to the silver mines in Peru, but the outbreak of a series of revolutions there left him without funds once again. Trevithick remained for a time in South America, pearl fishing in Panama, mineral prospecting, and fighting in the Latin American wars of liberation alongside the revolutionary leader Simón Bolívar (1783–1830). Eventually Trevithick borrowed money to return home to England. Further schemes were no more successful, and in 1833 he died penniless. Nevertheless he wrote, shortly before his death, that he was "satisfied by the great secret pleasure and… pride" he felt when he thought of the machines he had invented.

WATT AND THE KETTLE

James Watt's fascination with steam seems to have begun at an early age, as we learn from this story, recorded by his cousin, Mrs. Campbell. "Sitting one evening with his aunt, Mrs. Muirhead, at the tea table, she said: 'James Watt, I never saw such an idle boy; take a book or employ yourself usefully; for the last hour you have not spoken a word, but taken off the lid of that kettle and put it on again, holding now a cup and now a silver spoon over the steam, watching how it rises from the spout, and catching and connecting the drops of hot water it falls into. Are you not ashamed of spending your time this way?'"

but he soon saw that a problem with Newcomen's basic design meant that the engine would not keep going for long. Steam was being wasted because the cylinder was losing too much heat through the walls, and so the engine came quickly to a stop. Watt decided he could improve the efficiency of the Newcomen engine by introducing a second chamber in which the steam could be condensed. This would allow the working cylinder to keep its heat throughout the process. Watt himself believed that, "As steam was an elastic fluid it would rush into a vessel and might there be condensed without cooling the cylinder." It was an ingenious solution to the problem.

THE ATMOSPHERIC ENGINE

The first patented steam engine was developed in 1698 by English engineer Thomas Savery (c. 1650–1715), who had created an engine he called the "Miner's Friend" because it was used to pump water out of mines. However, in 1712 a better engine was designed by Thomas Newcomen, an ironmonger working in the mines of Cornwall in southwest England. In Newcomen's engine, water is heated in a boiler to produce steam. This passes into a cylinder containing a piston (a sliding piece). The hot steam expands within the cylinder, pushing the piston up. Cold water is then injected into the cylinder, cooling the steam, which condenses into water. Because a cubic foot of steam condenses into only one cubic inch of water, a partial vacuum (a space empty of air) is created in the cylinder. As air pushes into the top of the cylinder to fill the vacuum, the atmospheric pressure forces the piston down.

   The piston is connected to a rocking beam. From the other side of the beam a pump handle runs down into the mineshaft. As the piston falls, pulling one side of the beam down toward it, the beam on the other side rises, working the pump and drawing water from the shaft. A Newcomen engine could produce about 12 strokes a minute. The engine was a marvel of its time, yet because it needed to heat water and then cool the steam every stroke, it consumed a lot of fuel. In 1765 Watt's simple adaptation of the Newcomen engine—adding a separate condenser so that the cylinder remained hot and the condenser stayed cool throughout the operation—cut the cost of fueling the steam engine by 75 percent.

ATMOSPHERE IN ACTION

Watt's engine was the culmination of centuries of experimentation and design. People long ago were using air (the atmosphere) to perform various tasks, even if they were not aware of it. For example, suction pumps had been used since Roman times to raise water, but it took Italian physicist Evangelista

Torricelli (1608–1647) to explain how they worked.

Suction pumps are made up of a cylinder enclosing a piston. When the piston is raised, a partial vacuum is created, and atmospheric pressure pushes water into the cylinder. The water then escapes through an outlet and the process is repeated. It was known that pumps could lift water no more than 32 feet (9.75 m): to raise water higher than this, two or more pumps are needed on successive levels. Torricelli showed this was because the weight of the atmosphere and the weight of the water in the cylinder are in balance at this height, so that the water cannot be lifted any higher.

Torricelli predicted that if the atmosphere had to balance a heavier liquid, the liquid would reach a much lower height. This was confirmed in 1643 by his pupil Vincenzo Viviani (1622–1703), who showed that mercury (which is 14 times heavier than water) would stand 14 times lower, that is only 28 inches (71 cm). It was clear from these experiments that the atmosphere had power. In 1650 German engineer and physicist Otto von Guericke (1602–1686) performed an impressive experiment in front of the emperor Ferdinand III (1608–1657). He joined together two large copper hemispheres, and pumped out the air inside them to create a vacuum. Von Guericke then arranged for two teams of eight horses to try and pull the hemispheres apart. To the amazement of observers, they failed. This was because there was no pressure inside the hemispheres; the only force acting on them was the external weight, or pressure, of the atmosphere, amounting to 15 pounds per square inch (6.8 kg per 6.5 sq. cm). When air reentered the hemispheres, they fell apart by themselves.

WATT'S PARTNERS

To develop his engine commercially, Watt needed financing, business skills, and access to a big engineering works. In 1768 he entered into partnership with John Roebuck (1718–1794), the owner of an ironworks. The following year Watt took out a patent for his new steam engine. A patent is a government licence that allows an inventor—for a limited time—to be the only person to make, use, and sell his or her invention. Watt's patent was for "A New Invented Method of Lessening the Consumption of Steam and Fuel in Fire Engines."

In 1773 Roebuck went bankrupt, and sold his interest in Watt's engine to English engineer Matthew Boulton (1728–1809), the owner of a large manufacturing business in Birmingham. Boulton was a man of vision, who could see the great opportunities for trade in the Industrial Revolution that was just beginning in England. He spoke of "serving the World with Engines of all sizes." Watt's partnership with Boulton lasted 25 years and gave him the financial backing to make rapid progress with his engine.

POWERING A REVOLUTION

The Industrial Revolution was the period when Western societies changed from an agricultural, handicraft economy to one based on industry and the production of machine-made goods. It had its beginnings in Britain in the late 18th century and gathered pace from the 1830s, spreading to continental Europe and the United States. Important elements of the revolution were new inventions and new methods of producing and transporting goods.

THE TEXTILE INDUSTRY

The effects of the Industrial Revolution were first felt in the cotton and woolen industries of northern England. New machinery, such as the spinning jenny invented by James Hargreaves (c. 1720–1778), a waterpowered spinning frame invented by Richard Arkwright (1732–1792), and the spinning mule invented by Samuel Crompton (1753–1827) in 1779, had greatly improved the speed and efficiency of weaving cloth. Before these improvements, cloth manufacturers would distribute the raw materials for spinning and weaving to workers to be made into cloth on simple spinning wheels and handlooms at home. The new machines, however, were far too big to be accommodated in small buildings, so gradually cloth manufacturers built large "factories," to which people had to travel, and in which they had to work every day—the beginnings of mass production.

STEAM POWER

At about the same time as these developments were taking place, iron manufacture was transformed by the development of the blast furnace. As a result, iron founders such as Abraham Darby (1711–1763) were able to manufacture large numbers of cast-iron cylinders for the new steam engines developed by Newcomen and Watt that were speeding up the pace of industrial change still further. Watermills and windmills relied on unpredictable elements (water can freeze and wind can stop blowing), while the steam engine did not need such external resources in order to work. Engineers gradually gained the skills to build more reliable machines; the development of machine tools such as lathes and steam hammers meant that much more accurate machine parts were produced.

A REVOLUTION IN TRANSPORT

Coal was essential for these processes, so industrial centers grew up around coalfields. A network of canals was built to carry raw materials to the new manufacturing cities such as Manchester and Birmingham, and to transport manufactured goods to London and the port cities. By 1815, there were more than 2,200 miles (3,540 km) of waterways in Britain. It was the railroads that saw the greatest growth, however. In Britain the first public railroad using locomotive traction to carry goods and passengers was opened between Stockton and Darlington in northeast England in 1825, and by 1841 there were more than 1,300 miles (2,000 km) of tracks in Britain. The first railroad in the United States began operating between Baltimore and Ellicott City in Maryland in 1830. Bulk freight, however, was mostly carried by steamboat along the Mississippi and other great rivers.

THE INDUSTRIAL REVOLUTION SPREADS

For a while Britain—at war with France for much of the time between 1792 and 1815, and guarding its lead in the Industrial Revolution—did not allow the export of machines, workers, or manufacturing processes to Europe. Spies were even sent to Britain to try and extract technical information! As peace returned after the Napoleonic wars, industrial knowledge and techniques gradually spread to countries such as Belgium, France, Switzerland, and Germany. By 1870 most continental European countries could compete with Britain. In the United States industrial development began in the late 1870s: the number of workers in industry doubled between 1880 and 1900. As elsewhere, the rapid expansion of the railroad system created a huge demand for steel; the Scottish-born American industrialist Andrew Carnegie (1835–1918) built the largest iron and steel works in the United States and earned himself a multimillion-dollar fortune.

Using a spinning jenny, one worker could produce eight spools of yarn at once.

REFINING THE DESIGN

Watt's patent was extended by the British government, and from 1776 many of his engines were installed to pump water from mines, particularly in the copper and tin mines of Cornwall. Boulton began to encourage Watt to replace the action of the original machine, which used an up-and-down motion known to engineers as "reciprocating." With this type of motion energy is used first to accelerate the piston and then to stop it. As any bicyclist knows, this wastes energy: much less effort is needed to keep a bicycle moving forward at a steady speed—by turning your legs in a circle (rotary motion)—than to get it

moving after a stop by pumping your legs up and down. The simplest way to produce rotary motion is by using a crank, such as those used, for example, in modern car engines. The crank converts the reciprocating motion of the cylinders into the circular motion of the car's wheels. Unfortunately for Watt, a patent on the crank had already been awarded in 1780 to another inventor. So instead of using a crank, Watt created a number of alternative linking devices, including the sun-and-planet gear wheel, which transformed up-and-down motion into rotary motion.

In Watt's original design for his steam engine, steam operated on one side of the piston only. In 1782 he patented a method to allow steam to be admitted and condensed on both sides of the piston, so doubling the engine's output by producing power on both the up and the down strokes of the piston. The engine needed a new method of securing the piston to the beam. Watt solved the problem with an arrangement of rods that he described as "one of the most ingenious, simple pieces of mechanism I have contrived."

In 1794 Watt and Boulton set up the firm of Boulton & Watt and built a factory called the Soho Foundry for making steam engines more efficiently. Watt's patents were due to run out in 1800, after which other people could build steam engines, so he wanted to prepare for the competition.

Sun-and-planet gear wheels convert vertical motion into circular motion.

OLIVER EVANS 1755-1819

The son of a farmer, Oliver Evans was born in the American colonies, in Newport, Delaware. His interest in steam power derived from a book he read describing the Newcomen engine. At this time there were no more than four or five engines in the country. Evans began to think about using high-pressure steam to drive vehicles as early as 1777, and in 1812 he made what seemed a very unlikely prediction: that one day a man would be able to leave Washington in the morning and arrive in New York on the same day. In the beginning Evans found it easier to adapt his engines for work in mills. In 1785 he installed the first continuous production line in a flour mill. This is a time-saving system in which component parts are carried through a number of different machine or human-operated processes. Evans's mill was driven by water power, which was also used to grind the corn and carry the grain through the mill by way of a system of elevators, hoppers, and belts, "without the aid of human labor." Evans later built steamboats. He launched the first, named the *Oliver Evans*, in 1816. Like Watt and other steam pioneers, much of Evans's later life was spent in court defending patents and pursuing the pirates who infringed his rights.

In 1794 his son James and Boulton's son Matthew took over the running of the company. By 1800 Boulton and Watt's company had built about 500 engines, most of which were of the rotary motion type. The engines soon became used by a range of industries.

HIGH-PRESSURE ENGINES

Watt's engines, which worked at low temperatures and low steam pressures, were large and cumbersome. Higher steam pressure, produced at greater temperatures, would raise the energy efficiency of the engine, but Watt thought that "strong steam," as he termed it, was dangerous, bringing the risk of explosions. He refused to work on the development of high-pressure engines, and because the terms of his steam engine patent were so broad, no one else could develop them either. Patents, and their vigilant enforcement, are often seen as barriers to progress. Watt's opposition to high-pressure engines prevented other inventors from developing an improved steam engine for about 20 years.

Richard Trevithick (1771–1833) was an enthusiast for high-pressure engines. In 1801, a year after Watt's patent ran out, he built his first steam carriage, which he drove up a hill in Cornwall, and in 1802 took out a patent for high-pressure engines for stationary and locomotive use. Trevithick had developed an ingenious safety measure against explosions. A safety valve on the boiler did not always guarantee protection; workers often screwed the valves down to make the machines easier to operate, increasing the risk of explosion. Trevithick's answer

Richard Trevithick spent some of his career working as a mining consultant in Peru.

was to use lead rivets; these melted when the water reached a certain temperature, allowing steam to escape.

Watt's engines, with huge cylinders 7 feet (2 m) in diameter, were far too unwieldy to be used for transportation; the great advantage of Trevithick's high-pressure engine was that it was smaller, lighter, and more efficient in fuel and energy. By 1804, Trevithick had built the first steam-powered locomotive and used it to haul a load of iron and 70 men a distance of 10 miles (16 km). Trevithick was a talented engineer who made many improvements to boiler design and construction. But although his high-pressure engine was to prove highly versatile, it brought him no financial profit.

GOOD BUSINESS

Trevithick's lack of business sense was in marked contrast to Watt, who made a considerable amount of money from his invention. However, Watt was forced to spend time and money in court to defend his patents against what he called "pirates." Watt's engines were first used in collieries and ironworks. His firm, Boulton & Watt, designed and supervised the building of the engine, while the customer paid the material and building costs. Profits were calculated on a basis of how much fuel their clients saved by using one of their machines: "if we save nothing we shall take nothing," they assured customers. A different method of payment was devised for the rotary engine, which operated mills of various kinds, from cotton to grain. Watt worked out that a horse, the previous source of mill power, could raise 33,000 pounds by one foot in one minute (14,969 kg by 0.3 m in one minute), a measure Watt called horsepower, or hp. The mill owners paid a charge based on how many horsepower per year were provided by Watt's rotary engines.

LATER YEARS

Watt was married twice: first to his cousin Margaret Miller, with whom he had six children. Three years after her death in 1773 he married Ann MacGregor, with whom he had two more children. He had a wide interest in instrument-making and scientific invention, and when he retired in 1800, he fitted out the garret of his home, Heathfield Hall near Birmingham, as a workshop. He died there on August 25, 1819, aged 83.

SCIENTIFIC BACKGROUND

Before 1740

Evangelista Torricelli (1608–1647) explains how atmospheric pressure works to raise water using pumps; Otto von Guericke (1602–1686) demonstrates atmospheric pressure using two hemispheres

English engineer Thomas Savery (c. 1650–1715) patents first steam engine; Thomas Newcomen (1663–1729) uses atmospheric pressure to drive his 1712 steam engine

1740

1744 American scientist and statesman Benjamin Franklin (1706–1790) invents the Franklin stove, which uses hot air to heat a room

1747 The first civil engineering school, the School for Bridges and Highways, is established in France

1750

1752 English engineer James Brindley (1716–1772) devises a water engine for draining a coal mine

1760

1764 James Hargreaves (c.1720–1778) invents the spinning jenny, which can spin many threads at the same time

1765 James Watt builds the first model of his steam engine with separate condenser

1770

1770

1769 English industrialist Richard Arkwright (1732–1792) invents a spinning frame that produces a strong warp thread

1774 English inventor and manufacturer John Wilkinson (1728–1808) develops a machine that can bore cylinders for Boulton & Watt's steam engines

1779 The first cast-iron bridge in the world is built at Coalbrookdale, England

1780

1782 Watt patents his double-acting steam engine

1785 English inventor Edmund Cartwright (1743–1823) builds the first power loom

1790

1800 English engineer Richard Trevithick (1771–1833) builds his first high-pressure steam engine

1800

1804 Trevithick's latest steam locomotive carries 10 tons of iron over 10 miles (16 km)

1807 The first practical, economical steamboat, the *Clermont*, is built by American engineer Robert Fulton (1765–1815); it makes its maiden voyage from Manhattan to Clermont, NY.

1810

1814 English engineer George Stephenson (1781–1848) develops his first steam engine

1820

After 1820

1885 German engineer Gottlieb Daimler (1834–1900) builds a motor car that uses a high-speed internal combustion engine

1897 The first practical compression-ignition engine, developed by German engineer Rudolph Diesel (1858–1913), has an efficiency twice that of similar steam engines

POLITICAL AND CULTURAL BACKGROUND

1731 American statesman and scientist Benjamin Franklin (1706–1790) sets up the first circulating library in North America

1738 Excavations begin near Naples in southern Italy to uncover the Roman city of Herculaneum, buried under volcanic ash after the eruption of Mount Vesuvius in 79 AD

1749 The College of Philadelphia is founded; it will later become the University of Pennsylvania

1752 Britain and the American colonies finally transfer from the old Julian calendar to the Gregorian calendar, devised in 1582; the old calendar has fallen 11 days behind the new

1763 The area of Canada still under French rule is passed over to the English under the Treaty of Paris

1765 The Stamp Act, passed by the British Parliament, taxes items such as newspapers, dice, and playing cards, and is the first direct tax to be imposed on the American colonists

1775 In Britain, bond labor by women and children is ended in salt and coal mines

1781 The American Revolution ends on October 19, though the British continue to hold New York until 1783

1787 George Washington (1732–1799) chairs the constitutional convention in Philadelphia that formulates a constitution for the newly created United States of America

1789 George Washington becomes the first chief-magistrate or president of the new United States government

1799 Napoleon Bonaparte (1769–1812) overthrows the French government and becomes established as first consul of France

1799 In Washington, D.C., the U S executive mansion is completed; in 1814 it is rebuilt and repainted after being burned down by British troops and is renamed the White House

1811 The first major novel by English writer Jane Austen (1775–1817), *Sense and Sensibility*, is published anonymously in London

1813 In Britain, leaders of the Luddite movement — textile workers who smash the new looms they fear will put them out of work—are hanged or transported to Australia

1821 Napoleon dies on the island of Saint Helena in the south Atlantic, having been exiled there in 1815

absolute temperature scale The temperature scale that begins at absolute zero. It is also called the Kelvin temperature scale.

absolute zero The lowest temperature possible (equal to −273°C).

alcohol thermometer A type of liquid-in-glass thermometer in which the expansion of a column of alcohol (dyed red or blue) along a narrow tube indicates temperature.

atom The smallest part of a chemical element that can exist on its own. It has a central nucleus (made up of protons and neutrons), surrounded by electrons.

bimetallic strip A strip consisting of two different metals bonded together. The metals have different coefficients of expansion, so the strip bends when it is heated.

black body A theoretical object that is a perfect absorber and emitter of heat radiation.

calorie (cal) A unit of heat equal to the amount of heat needed to raise the temperature of 1 gram of water through 1°C.

Calorie (with a capital C) 1,000 calories, the same as a kilocalorie.

Celsius scale A temperature scale that has 100 degrees between the freezing point of water (0°C) and the boiling point of water (100°C). It used to be called the centigrade scale.

centigrade scale An old name for the Celsius scale.

change of state The change that takes place when, for example, a solid melts (and turns into a liquid) or a liquid boils (and turns into a gas or vapor). See also *latent heat*.

clinical thermometer A type of short mercury thermometer used for taking a person's temperature.

coefficient of expansion Also called expansivity, a measure of how much a substance expands when it is heated.

coefficient of linear expansion Also called linear expansivity, a measure of how much the length of a solid object increases when it is heated.

coefficient of volume expansion Also called volume expansivity, a measure of how much the volume of a substance (solid, liquid, or gas) increases when it is heated.

combustion Also commonly called burning, a type of chemical reaction that is accompanied by the production of heat (and often flames and light). When a fuel is combusted, its chemical energy is converted into heat energy.

condensation The process by which a gas or vapor changes into a liquid. The liquid formed is also sometimes called condensation.

conduction The process by which heat moves through a solid object. (In electricity conduction is the process by which an electric current moves through a substance.)

convection The usual way in which heat moves through a fluid (a liquid or gas) by setting up convection currents in the fluid.

convection current Movement of a fluid (a liquid or gas) that results when warm fluid rises and cold fluid flows in to take its place.

critical temperature The temperature above which a gas cannot be liquefied by pressure alone.

cryogenics The scientific study of very low temperatures.

digital thermometer A type of thermometer on which temperature is indicated directly by numbers on a liquid crystal display.

electromagnetic radiation Any type of radiation that travels at the speed of light. It includes, in order of decreasing wavelength, radio waves, microwaves, infrared radiation, visible light, ultraviolet radiation, X-rays, and gamma rays.

evaporation The changing of a liquid into a gas or vapor below its boiling point (caused by molecules escaping from its surface).

Fahrenheit scale A temperature scale that has 180 degrees between the freezing point of water (32°F) and the boiling point of water (212°F).

fluid A gas or a liquid.

friction A force that prevents or slows the movement of one surface against another surface. It results in the production of heat.

fusion The change from solid to liquid on heating; another word for melting. See *latent heat*.

gas A state of matter in which the molecules move at random. A gas in a container takes on the size and shape of the container.

geothermal energy A form of heat energy that comes from deep underground, as in geysers, hot springs, and volcanoes.

greenhouse effect An increase in temperature near the Earth's surface caused by heat energy trapped by gases in the atmosphere. Water vapor and carbon dioxide (from human activity) are the chief greenhouse gases.

heat The internal energy of an object that results from the vibrations of its particles (atoms or molecules).

heat capacity The amount of heat needed to raise the temperature of an object by 1°C. See also *specific heat capacity*.

heat engine A machine in which heat energy is converted into mechanical energy (for doing useful work). The heat energy itself comes from the combustion of a fuel.

infrared radiation Heat energy emitted by any object whose temperature is above absolute zero. The hotter it is, the more it radiates. See also *electromagnetic radiation*.

insulator A substance that is a poor conductor of heat (see *conduction*). In electricity an insulator is a substance that is a poor conductor of electric current.

joule (J) The SI unit of energy, equal to the amount of work done when a force of 1 newton acts through a distance of 1 meter.

Joule–Kelvin effect Another name for the Joule–Thomson effect.

Joule–Thomson effect Also called the Joule–Kelvin effect, the cooling of a gas that takes place when it escapes through a narrow hole. The effect is important in a refrigerator.

Kelvin temperature scale See *absolute temperature scale*.

kilocalorie (kcal) 1,000 calories, sometimes called a Calorie (with a capital C).

latent heat The heat taken in or given out when a substance undergoes a change of state. The latent heat of fusion is the heat needed to change a solid at its melting point into a liquid (and is the same as the latent heat of freezing). The latent heat of vaporization is the heat needed to change a liquid at its boiling point into a vapor (and is the same as the latent heat of condensation).

latent heat of fusion See *latent heat*.

latent heat of vaporization See *latent heat*.

linear expansivity Another name for the coefficient of linear expansion.

liquid A state of matter, between a gas and a solid, that has a level surface and, below that surface, takes on the shape of its container.

liquid-in-glass thermometer A type of thermometer in which temperature is indicated by the expansion of a column of liquid along a narrow tube, which is graduated in the degrees of a temperature scale.

maximum-and-minimum thermometer A type of thermometer that has two temperature scales, one indicating the highest temperature reached and one indicating the lowest temperature reached over a period of time.

mercury thermometer A type of liquid-in-glass thermometer in which the expansion of a column of mercury along a narrow tube indicates temperature.

molecule A combination of at least two atoms that forms the smallest independent unit of a chemical element or compound.

platinum resistance thermometer A type of thermometer that measures temperature in terms of the electrical resistance of a length of platinum (making use of the known relationship between temperature and the resistance of platinum).

pyrometer An instrument for measuring very high temperatures.

radiation The process by which heat is emitted by any object whose temperature is above absolute zero, usually in the form of infrared radiation. Infrared radiation can travel through a vacuum. See also *electromagnetic radiation*.

resistance A measure of how a material or a component resists the passage of electric current through it.

solid A state of matter that keeps its own shape (unlike a gas or a liquid).

specific heat capacity The amount of heat needed to raise the temperature of 1 kilogram of a substance by 1°C. See also *heat capacity*.

sublimation A change of state in which a substance turns directly from a solid into a gas or vapor (without first melting).

superconductivity A property of some metals at very low temperatures when they have no electrical resistance.

superfluidity A property of some substances at very low temperatures when they have no viscosity.

temperature The degree of hotness (or coldness) of an object.

temperature scale A scale of numbers, called degrees, for expressing how hot or cold something is. See also *absolute temperature scale*; *Celsius scale*; *Fahrenheit scale*.

thermal A vertical convection current in a gas, usually air.

thermal conductivity A measure of the ability of a substance to conduct heat.

thermic lance A tool that consists of a tube of steel rods through which oxygen is pumped. The metal burns at temperatures of over 3,000°C (5,400°F) and can be used for cutting through steel or concrete.

thermocouple An electrical device for measuring temperature. It has two wires of different metals joined at their ends. When the joins are at different temperatures, an electric current flows in the wires and can be measured with a sensitive voltmeter, which displays the temperature difference between the joins.

thermograph A picture that shows heat patterns—the different temperatures of an object or scene—as different colors.

thermometer An instrument for measuring temperature. There are various types, such as the clinical thermometer, liquid-in-glass thermometer, maximum-and-minimum thermometer, and platinum resistance thermometer.

thermostat A device for maintaining a constant temperature, consisting of a temperature-sensitive element (such as a bimetallic strip) that controls the electricity or fuel supply to a heater.

vapor Another name for the gas that forms when a liquid boils or evaporates.

vaporization The change from liquid to gas or vapor on heating. See *latent heat*.

viscosity A measure of how easily a liquid flows (that is, how "thick" it is).

volume expansivity Another name for the coefficient of volume expansion.

American Meteorological Society
45 Beacon Street
Boston, MA 02108
617-227-2425
Web site: http://www.ametsoc.org
This organization promotes research
    and sharing of information on the
    atmosphere and related sciences.
    The AMS publishes print and online
    journals and sponsors several confer-
    ences each year.

California State Railroad Museum
125 "I" Street
Sacramento, CA 95814
916-445-6645
Web site: http://www.csrmf.org/
This museum complex includes the
    Railroad History Museum, which
    features 21 restored locomotives and
    cars. Exhibits highlight how locomo-
    tives and railroads shaped California
    and the American West.

Geothermal Energy Association
209 Pennsylvania Ave SE
Washington, DC 20003
202-454-5261
Web site: http://www.geo-energy.org/
This trade organization is made up of
    companies who want to expand the
    use of geothermal energy in the
    United States.

Hawaii Volcanoes National Park
P.O. Box 52
Hawaii National Park, HI 96718
808-985-6000
Web site: http://www.nps.gov/havo/
    index.htm
At this national park, located on the Big
    Island of Hawaii, visitors can experi-
    ence the heat of an active volcano
    and explore the paths of prior
    eruptions.

Science Museum
Exhibition Road, South
Kensington, London, SW7 2dd
United Kingdom
+44 (0)20 7942 4000
Web site: http://www.sciencemuseum.
    org.uk/
This museum in the United Kingdom
    has an area called the Energy Hall,
    which houses an exhibit on James
    Watt and his steam engine.

Steamship Historical Society of America
30C Kenney Drive
Cranston, RI 02920
401-463-3570
Web site: https://www.sshsa.org
This group, formed in 1935, is dedicated
    to recording, preserving, and sharing
    the history of engine-powered ves-
    sels. They have a collection of
    hundreds of thousands images, offi-
    cial records, and artifacts related to
    engine-powered vessels, and publish
    a magazine called *PowerShips*.

Steamtown National Historic Site
150 South Washington Avenue
Scranton, PA 18503
570-340-5200
Web site: http://www.nps.gov/stea/
    index.htm
At this national park, visitors can experi-
    ence the era of steam. There is a
    Technology Museum, History
    Museum, and visitors can even ride
    on a steam-powered locomotive.

World Nuclear Association
22a St. James's Square
London SW1Y 4JH
United Kingdom
+44 (0)20 7451 1520
Web site: http://www.world-nuclear.org/
This organization, based in the United
    Kingdom, represents people and
    organizations involved in nuclear
    power around the world. Their Web
    site includes basic information on
    nuclear power as well as charts, out-
    lines, and scientific papers with
    up-to-date information about nuclear
    power.

WEB SITES

Due to the changing nature of Internet
links, Rosen Publishing has developed
an online list of Web sites related to the
subject of this book. This site is updated
regularly. Please use this link to access
the list:

http://www.rosenlinks.com/CORE/Heat

Alfred, Randy, *Mad Science: Einstein's Fridge, Dewar's Flask, Mach's Speed, and 362 Other Inventions and Discoveries that Made Our World*. New York: Little, Brown and Company, 2013.

Archer, David. *Global Warming: Understanding the Forecast*. Hoboken, NJ: Wiley Publishing, 2012.

Biddle, Wayne. *A Field Guide to Radiation*. New York: Penguin Books, 2012.

Faust, Daniel R. *Global Warming: Greenhouse Gases and the Ozone Layer*. Jr. Graphic Environmental Dangers. New York: PowerKids Press, 2009.

Gale, Robert Peter, and Eric Lax. *Radiation: What It Is, What You Need to Know*. New York: Vintage Books, 2014.

Gray, Theodore. *The Elements: A Visual Exploration of Every Known Atom in the Universe*. New York: Black Dog and Leventhal Publishers, 2012.

Hayes, Allyson E. *Cryogenics: Theory, Processes and Applications. Physics Research and Technology*. Hauppauge, NY: Nova Science Publishers, 2011.

Klein, Sanford, and Gregory Nellis. *Thermodynamics*. Cambridge, UK: Cambridge University Press, 2012.

Lankford, Ronnie. *Greenhouse Gases*. At Issue: Environment. Farmington Hills, MI: Greenhaven Press, 2009.

Marsden, Ben. *Watt's Perfect Engine: Steam and the Age of Invention. Revolutions in Science*. New York: Columbia University Press, 2004.

Nellis, Gregory, and Sanford Klein. *Heat Transfer*. Cambridge, UK: Cambridge University Press, 2009.

Osborne, Roger. *Iron, Steam, & Money: The Making of the Industrial Revolution*. New York: Vintage Digital, 2013.

Reynolds, Osborne. *Biography of James Prescott Joule*. History of Physics. Palm Springs, CA: Wexford College Press, 2007.

Rhodes, Richard. *The Making of the Atomic Bomb*. Simon & Schuster, 2012.

Thipse, S. S. *Cryogenics: A Textbook*. Oxford, UK: Alpha Science International, 2013.

Turns, Stephen. *An Introduction to Combustion: Concepts and Applications*. New York: McGraw-Hill, 2011.

Weeks, Daniel. *Pushing Electrons*. Independence, KY: Cengage Learning, 2013.

Whiting, Jim. *James Watt and the Steam Engine*. Uncharted, Unexplored, and Unexplained. Hockessin, DE: Mitchell Lane Publishers, 2006.

PHOTO CREDITS